CORE CURRICULUM AND CULTURAL PLURALISM

A GUIDE FOR CAMPUS PLANNERS

BETTY SCHMITZ
UNIVERSITY OF WASHINGTON/
WASHINGTON CENTER FOR UNDERGRADUATE
EDUCATION AT EVERGREEN STATE COLLEGE

FOREWORD BY
CAROL G. SCHNEIDER
EXECUTIVE VICE PRESIDENT
ASSOCIATION OF AMERICAN COLLEGES

PROJECT ON ENGAGING CULTURAL LEGACIES:
SHAPING CORE CURRICULA IN THE HUMANITIES
Carol G. Schneider, Director
Maria Helena Price, Assistant Director

ASSOCIATION OF AMERICAN COLLEGES, 1992

Published by
Association of American Colleges
1818 R Street, NW
Washington, DC 20009

Copyright 1992

ISBN 0-911696-57-1
Library of Congress Catalog Card No. 92-71980

CONTENTS

Foreword

This book reports on two remarkable aspects of the current wave of general-education reform: the creation or revival of common or "core" courses within general-education curricula and the emergence of cultural complexity and multiplicity as organizing themes in these new—or newly revised—core programs.

Rapid change both within and beyond the borders of the United States has engaged our society in a major renegotiation of the interpretations, stories, and artistic exemplars that constitute our public and private cultures. Faculty members at colleges and universities across the United States have set themselves the task of designing curricula that broaden traditional notions of "our common cultural heritage" to incorporate the plurality of cultures around the world and, increasingly, within the United States. Scores of colleges and universities are creating, restoring, or redesigning common learning experiences for undergraduate students; in doing so, they are redefining what is central to the education of these students, whose lives and careers will span the first half of the twenty-first century.

These changes have fostered a curricular renaissance in American higher education. This guidebook for curriculum planners analyzes that emerging renaissance. It demonstrates why colleges and universities view these new cultural legacies core courses as important priorities. It also outlines the kinds of questions faculties must address in framing and sustaining core programs.

This book draws on the Association of American Colleges' project, Engaging Cultural Legacies: Shaping Core Curricula in the Humanities. Funded by two grants from the National Endowment for the Humanities, the project has made possible a unique collaborative dialogue among sixty-three institutions engaged in core curriculum development or revision.* The eleven "resource institutions" in the project have provided consultation, guidance, and a family of curricular models for the rest of the

---

*Two groups of "planning institutions" were selected through national competitions to participate in the project: twenty-seven colleges and universities in 1990 and another twenty-seven in 1991. Each of these two groups worked with nine "resource institutions." Two institutions that had been planning institutions in the first round served as resource institutions for the second round.

project. The fifty-four "planning institutions" are at various points in the cycle of core program planning, conceptualization, and implementation: Most are designing or piloting new courses for a cultural legacies sequence; some are implementing previously piloted courses for all their students; a few are redesigning long-established core programs in the humanities and/or the study of civilizations.

Significantly, the project's initial distinction between resource and planning institutions has been largely blurred in practice. All of the resource institutions are themselves engaged in adapting or significantly revising their core programs to engage the complexities of the contemporary world. Moreover, the planning institutions include several widely recognized as leaders in core curriculum who also are revising their core programs. The message of these examples is that, across the country, faculty members are rethinking what students need to know in a world newly cognizant both of its cultural multiplicity and of its fundamental interdependence.

CURRICULAR DIALOGUES

Those encountering debates about the curriculum only through the popular or academic press might naturally conclude that the discussions are both impossibly contentious and largely stalemated. If we turn away from the media mirrors, however, to observe what actually is happening on campuses, we see not division and impasse but exciting curricular dialogue and invention. Eschewing "the West versus multiculturalism" of the unhappy public debate, faculties across the country are developing new general-education courses that see diversity—in both culture and perspective—as an integral dimension of any intellectually rigorous encounter with either "Western" or "world" civilizations.

The institutions in the Cultural Legacies project are rethinking the once-standard model for Western civilization courses and programs. They are finding ways to enrich and extend its boundaries, to connect it with world studies, to include in it more attention to the American hemisphere and the United States than was once standard. Virtually all see demanding texts—from all cultures, including, of course, the West—as integral to their educational goals. In selecting these texts, however, they are placing new emphasis on multiplicity, cultural pluralism, and cultural interaction—both as subjects in themselves and as resources to help undergraduates grasp the texture of the world they inhabit.

As the course syllabi described in this guide illustrate, the study of cultural pluralism in the United States and the world is too vast, faculty members' knowledge bases too diverse, and the potential pedagogical resources too various to create a single, common content paradigm. For earlier generations of Western civilization courses, a view of history as the evolution of human freedom provided organizing course themes, suggested a family of texts, and pointed toward particular historical epochs: fifth-century Athens, Renaissance Italy, seventeenth-century England, and the like. While such courses varied in detail, all were recognizably part of the same interpretation. There is no comparable overarching content principle visible across the new courses. Almost all make use of culture—patterns and webs of human meaning—as organizing principles. The patterns and webs encompassed in these courses, however, are as various as the institutions in which they are being developed.

CURRICULAR PLANNING

The complexity of this type of curricular reform is daunting. Each institution in AAC's project simultaneously faces two kinds of challenges. By deciding to make some version of "cultural legacies" the subject of a core program, colleges and universities confront the intellectually and institutionally tangled task of determining what such a commitment means in this complicated period in the evolution of American, Western, and world history. By deciding to offer its cultural legacies sequence as a common learning experiences for all students, an institution further commits itself to shaping a curriculum that can win widespread support—not only from faculty members and departments but also from students themselves.

Both faculties and students, of course, are notoriously resistant to the imposition of "required" studies. Yet 250 separate institutions sought places in AAC's project, some applying through two separate competitive selection processes, in 1990 and again in 1991. Dozens of other institutions are working on similar initiatives outside the framework of AAC's project.

We offer this guidebook both as a resource and as encouragement to other institutions to develop their own programs of common learning in history and culture. As these pages show, these kinds of curricula are important for students, for faculties, and for society at large.

Reaching consensus on a "core program" is difficult in any circumstance. It is especially difficult if there has not been a tradition of working together. Therefore, this guide places special emphasis on the "how" of creating a core program. It illustrates the crucial importance of faculty development and continued faculty learning—not just in the planning stage for a new program but as the key variable in sustaining a rich program in human culture and history. At the same time, as author Betty Schmitz makes clear, faculty commitment depends on judicious administrative commitment: a continuing set of signals and resources that make clear the value and significance of faculty members' investment in a new program.

Colleges and universities stand at an early point in the development of programs that explore cultural legacies and complexities at home and abroad. Internationally, we are going through this century's third major transformation of world relationships. Domestically, the United States is catapulting into a new self-consciousness about its evolution as a world society, peopled by citizens who trace their roots to all parts of the globe.

It is inevitable and imperative that faculty members find ways to help their students grasp and negotiate these transforming interrelationships. When they introduce these topics in programs of common learning, they communicate the central significance of these topics not just for the degree but for the larger society.

The renaissance in core studies was inspired by the strong and assertive stance taken in the 1980s by the National Endowment for the Humanities on the need for the revival of substantive core curricula. The Endowment has made resources available to dozens of institutions to undertake campus programs of faculty study and curriculum planning requisite to this revival. Both AAC and the institutions participating in both rounds of the Cultural Legacies project are indebted to NEH—and particularly to program officers Frank Frankfort and Lyn Maxwell White—for articulating many significant issues with which core curriculum planners engaging cultural legacies have grappled. NEH staff members encouraged and supported a project model that enabled institutions and individuals to share critical perspectives, insights, models, and information that have resulted in a substantial array of high quality humanities core programs.

This guide should be perused in conjunction with Jerry Gaff's new book, *New Life for the College Curriculum* (Jossey-Bass, 1992)—which gives a general overview of the context, process, and outcomes of current general education initiatives—and with *The Challenge of Connecting Learning*, Volume One of AAC's series on "Liberal Learning and the Arts and Sciences Major." Together, these three books introduce a new framework for undergraduate liberal learning curricula for the twenty-first century.

CAROL G. SCHNEIDER
Executive Vice President, Association of American Colleges

Acknowledgments

I want to thank especially Carol Schneider, executive vice president of AAC and director of the Cultural Legacies project, who significantly shaped my thinking about curriculum change and sharpened my understanding of both historical and contemporary educational practices. Her extensive knowledge of theory and practice guided me throughout the development of this guide. She provided ongoing direction, inspiration, and critical perspective. Her vision also inspired the Afterword.

I also extend special gratitude to Maria Helena Price, assistant director of programs at AAC and assistant director of the Cultural Legacies project, who has extensive knowledge of the inner workings of the project and who conveyed the richness of the campus experiences to me and guided me in selecting examples for the text. She provided research support and advice throughout the writing of the guide.

Those who hosted site visits for me and for Carol Schneider were generous with their time and wisdom: Leonard Grob, Jack Becker, and Jim Kuehl (Fairleigh Dickinson University), David Leary and David Evans (University of Richmond), Pauline Drake (Spelman College), Margaret Downes and Merritt Moseley (University of North Carolina at Asheville), Victoria Weiss (Oglethorpe University), Carole Brown and John Rakestraw (Wesleyan College), Jack Meacham and John Thorpe (SUNY–Buffalo), Karen Klein (Brandeis University), Marie T. Callahan (Massachusetts Bay Community College), and Richard Guarasci and Grant Cornwell (St. Lawrence University). I also am grateful to the consultants, listed in the Appendix, who wrote reports based on their site visits to the planning institutions and shared insights at meetings.

The readers of the various drafts of this guide provided careful and thoughtful guidance on many complex and difficult issues. I extend my appreciation to: Jerry Gaff, who also contributed substantially to the bibliography; Jack Meacham, Margaret Downes, Bari Watkins, John Thorpe, and Thomas Flynn, all colleagues in the Cultural Legacies project; Zee Gamson and Sandra Kanter from the New England Resource Center for Higher Education; Barbara Leigh Smith, director of the Washington Center for Undergraduate Education at Evergreen State College; and, finally, Johnnella Butler, for ten years of insights and wisdom about curricular change.

I wish to thank my editor, David Stearman, AAC's acting director of public information and publications, for his astute editing and sustained interest in this project since its inception. I am grateful also to Maureen McNulty, Ruth Futrovsky, and Kevin Hovland, who provided important research support at critical times.

I have benefited from judicious guidance and extensive support from these individuals; however, I bear sole responsibility for the final version of this text. Although this guide is based on an AAC project funded by the National Endowment for the Humanities, the conclusions expressed here do not necessarily reflect the opinions of AAC, NEH, or any of the individuals named above. Any errors of fact or interpretation are mine.

BETTY SCHMITZ
September 1992

Introduction

The Association of American Colleges' project, Engaging Cultural Legacies: Shaping Core Curricula in the Humanities, was well under way when I joined AAC as a Senior Fellow in June 1991 to write about the process of shaping core curricula in the humanities. The twenty-seven planning institutions in the first round of the project were completing their work; AAC staff members were making decisions about which institutions to fund for the second round. AAC's executive vice president, Carol Schneider, asked me to examine the experiences of the first round of planning institutions to see what elements of practice might be helpful for other institutions interested in redesigning or creating core programs to address cultural legacies. This guidebook is the result of my work.

Carol Schneider and her colleagues at AAC had designed a project to assist institutions in creating an *intentional* core curricular experience for undergraduate students. They recognized that in a time of rapid cultural transformation, college and university faculty members have the responsibility to provide students with the opportunity to address the complexity of historical and contemporary interactions within and among cultures. The Cultural Legacies project invited institutions to address this pressing curricular need in its local, national, and international dimensions while simultaneously reinvesting in core curricula as a foundation for undergraduate education.

Interestingly—and I believe significantly—cultural pluralism became a more significant aspect in the planning institutions' curricular initiatives than the project's designers first envisioned. As AAC Senior Fellow Robert Schoenberg reported in an analysis of the 191 applications to the first round of the Cultural Legacies project, "Institutions are seriously committed to using the general education curriculum to increase awareness of cultural diversity, both within the United States and among the peoples of the world and both historically and contemporarily....very few proposals were focused on strengthening courses exclusively in Western civilization."[1]

Among the twenty-seven planning institutions in the first round of the project, the majority envisioned core programs that would address world as well as Western cultural traditions. Moreover, the resource institutions—those serving as mentors to the planning institutions—were themselves increasing attention to cultural diversity in their core programs: sometimes by adding new materials on world cultures, sometimes by adding readings and course units on such topics in Western experience as anti-Semitism, racial conflict, gender constructs, or cross-cultural encounters.

The research for this book thus allowed me to study curriculum planning at a significant and transitional moment in higher education in the United States. The institutions selected for the Cultural Legacies project—and the nearly two hundred other applicants—all wished to create rich and demanding experiences of common learning for their students. They all wanted to develop core curricula responsive to the complexities and historic challenges of the contemporary world. As Carol Schneider notes in her Foreword, however, they made these commitments at a time when there was no dominant or widely agreed-upon model for engaging cultural multiplicity in a program of common study. Faculty members in the core programs I studied are drawing new curricular maps. The courses they teach are very much works-in-progress; each of these programs can be expected to evolve and change in the semesters and years ahead.

I brought to this project several of my own interests and perspectives. Having worked for more than ten years in curriculum change associated with the incorporation of new scholarship from women's studies and ethnic studies into the curriculum, I am particularly interested in how new ideas make their way onto a campus, what responses these ideas elicit, and how they succeed or fail to change the culture of an institution. I have observed change processes in many different kinds of programs that have attempted to do something with or to general education over the past decade and a half—the many and varied "across-the-curriculum" efforts that focus on both content and pedagodical issues: writing; computing and media-assisted instruction; international studies; collaborative learning; and ethnic and gender studies.

Many separate and sequential demands have been placed on general education over the past two decades. Too often, the result has been curricula with spotty attention to these various concerns and faculty members frustrated by multiple agendas. These earlier reform initiatives have, however, created faculty pockets of energy that could be readily tapped in this current effort to revitalize core curricula.

What I observed in the Cultural Legacies project were new alliances among faculty members and administrators who had had significant experiences with the earlier general-education curricular initiatives. Something more was going on in these projects than the creation and redesign of core curricula incorporating different cultural traditions: Core planners were using their varied and diverse experiences with curricular reform and faculty development to address a full range of issues that have plagued undergraduate education over the years.

Given this new level of expertise and new kinds of alliances in diverse and essential areas, it could be argued that for the first time in the recent history of general education, a coherent undergraduate experience is within reach. Administrators and faculty planners are benefiting from two decades of initiatives and experiments with improving general education and core studies, as well as from the numerous reports and studies by task forces, government agencies, and professional associations.[2]

Older concerns—basic skills, core studies, connected learning—take on new meaning when considered in conjunction with current issues such as global awareness, multicultural studies, and intercultural literacy. There is a sense of heightened urgency to curricular change associated with the rapidity of global political and socio-economic developments and with the anticipation of a new century. Demographic and fiscal imperatives add to this urgency. We are at a moment in time when we have the expertise to address persistent curricular issues and concerns and to move beyond cyclically recurring calls for reform to "changes of real consequence."[3] It remains to be seen if we have the will.

A NEW MODEL FOR THE CORE CURRICULUM

As a result of an intentional look at core study and its connections to other parts of the curriculum, the institutions I studied for this guide have achieved an integration of purposes and elements of general education that would not have been possible a decade ago. This book highlights current practices that constitute an emerging model for core curricula that includes *at its best*:

- rethinking of what students should know about Western traditions
- redefinition of core knowledge that includes study of U.S. pluralism and other parts of the world
- deliberate attempts to bring together administratively separate or competing curricular initiatives from the past two decades
- more attention to defining the kind and level of skills students are expected to acquire in specific courses and to the pedagogies that accomplish skill-related goals
- vertical sequencing of core curricula over three or four years of the undergraduate experience

- connecting learning across the disciplines and between the core curriculum and student life
- changes in the way faculty members think about their role in the teaching/learning equation
- changes in the way institutions think about the relationship between the core curriculum and the major.

Chapters 1 and 2 treat national trends that are discernible in the development of core curricula that address cultural pluralism, as well as issues and choices facing the participating institutions as they implement their core programs. I use examples from these institutions, with analytical commentary, to illustrate practice. There also are caveats and recommendations drawn from my analysis.

The division between content and pedagogy in Chapters 1 and 2 is both necessary and misleading. I address the content questions discretely because, for most faculty groups embarking on core curriculum planning, questions about how to envision course content are paramount. Challenging at any time, content questions have become especially charged because of the widespread interest in broadening and diversifying core curricula. On many campuses, moreover, faculty members hold more collective goals for core learning than can readily be incorporated in the amount of credit time available. These realities mean that course design will be a time-consuming and intellectually challenging activity for faculty planners.

Yet the separation of content is misleading because it is artificial. What is taught is inseparable from how it is taught. More importantly, as Chapter 2 suggests, the most effective programs are distinguished by their careful integration of intellectual goals with pedagogies thoughtfully designed to achieve them. Those planning core programs should expect to devote fully as much time to pedagogical decisions as to content questions.

Chapters 3 and 4 focus on the processes of faculty development and core curriculum implementation, respectively. Each of these chapters ends with a series of recommendations for good practice. Chapter 5 summarizes the characteristics of strong core programs that engage cultural pluralism, while the Afterword (co-authored by Carol Schneider) identifies challenges for the future. The book also includes syllabi, excerpts from core proposals, curriculum profiles, and lists of questions to guide campus planners.

ABOUT THE STUDY

I based this study on several kinds of data. The files on institutions participating in the first round of the Cultural Legacies project include excellent
records of the process of curriculum change at these institutions: the appli-
cation for participation; the reports of a consultant's site visit; the final
report, including the current course syllabi. Each document serves as a
snapshot of a moment in the institutional change process. Taken together,
they track and elucidate that process.

To gain deeper insight into the intellectual, political, and logistical
issues that impede and enhance curriculum change, Carol Schneider and I
made site visits to ten colleges and universities. Some were resource institutions in the project; others were first-round planning institutions. We spoke
with academic vice presidents, deans, core program directors, faculty members, and students in the programs. At most institutions, we attended core
faculty meetings or observed classes. For these visits, we chose both liberal
arts colleges and research universities; we also included several resource
institutions to gain perspectives on sustaining core programs over time.

In order to get a more consistent view of faculty ideas and opinions
about the new core courses, we surveyed faculty members at planning institutions from the first round of the project in which courses were being
taught and in which we did not meet a representative group of faculty members. We sent out a total of 110 questionnaires; we received responses from
70 faculty members representing twelve institutions. We discarded questionnaires from faculty members teaching courses fulfilling distribution requires
and were left with a sample of 48 faculty members from eleven institutions.

I also gathered data for this study through telephone interviews
with selected core directors and through attending two Cultural Legacies
project symposia: the initial meeting of the second-round institutions,
which featured many of the first-round institutions' stories and experiences,
and a meeting held in conjunction with AAC's 1992 Annual Meeting at
which many of the issues highlighted in this study were taken up.

In preparing this guide, I had available to me the ideas and insights
of the extensive network of individuals in the projects. Throughout the
text I quote from individuals I interviewed or heard speak on campus and
from institutional documents. Core planners were willing to share the ups
and downs of the process of designing and implementing core programs—
their problems and mistakes, as well as their successes. Their insights were
crucial to the development of my perspective on engaging cultural legacies
in core humanities curricula.

1 The Challenges of Content

▶ In the best core humanities programs, curricular decisions flow explicitly from goals for student learning.

▶ Programs that engage cultural pluralism in core curricula need not abandon the creation of a common experience; they can redefine a new commonality built from a diversity of cultural experiences.

CORE CURRICULA AND CULTURAL LEGACIES

Core, in the educational vernacular, means "essential," "fundamental," "central"; in the curricular vernacular, it means "required of all students." Throughout this century, there have been recurrent efforts to identify essential knowledge that all students should acquire and to design curricula to foster both common understandings and a shared sense of intellectual community. The current wave of core curriculum development is spurred in large part by concerns about fragmentation and lack of cohesiveness in the curriculum.

The 250 institutional authors who wrote applications to the Cultural Legacies project expressed deep concerns about fragmentation and great dissatisfaction with distribution requirements for their failure to provide connection across fields. Applicants described their current curricula as "not tightly structured," "not coherent," "disconnected bodies of knowledge"; they viewed a program of common study as a way to correct this fragmentation. From large institutions as well as small, the applications argued for the reinstatement or introduction of a discernible course of study—a humanities-based core—to provide an intellectual center for both students and faculty members.

The applications also testified, however, to another factor driving the revival of interest in common studies. Overwhelmingly, core planners described the importance of helping students locate themselves in a transformed and culturally diverse global community. Concerns over ethnocentrism echoed those of fragmentation. The increasing diversity of student bodies and the emergence of new scholarly fields of study, as well as the extraordinary global events surrounding the end of the Cold War, suggested a need for clarity in institutional approaches to cultural multiplicity.

In their proposals for core curricula, faculty members and administrators articulated plans for bringing together core and culture in ways that would serve students more effectively in today's context. The desire to have core studies and to focus these studies on cultural legacies thus brought curriculum planners inevitably into a confrontation with cultural multiplicity and issues of commonality and difference within the academy.

CULTURAL PLURALISM IN THE ACADEMY

College and university goal statements for liberal learning that refer to "our common cultural heritage" abound. In current efforts to reform core curricula, however, questions about who "we" are and what of "ours" is common to all are greatly contested. In attempting to forge a new commonality out of cultural multiciplicity, core planners in AAC's project found there was no common "we" to call upon. Elizabeth Kamarck Minnich (herself citing Hannah Arendt) illuminates this dilemma well:

> There is no one answer any more than there is any single foundation for a "we" within, on, or beneath which any of us can stand today unchallenged.... Even when we generally agree, we bring to the discussion differing perspectives, differing primary concerns, differing languages, and often our discussion is still more intense because some of us do not "generally agree": In academe as in public life, we are indeed "confronted anew...by the elementary problems of human living-together."[4]

Problems of commonality and difference play themselves out in questions about the place of traditional Western themes and texts in a core curriculum; where and how to include study of so-called non-Western cultures; where and how to include the study of U.S. pluralism or multiculturalism; and how to address race, gender, ethnicity, class, sexual orientation, and other constructed dimensions of human identity. The intensity of discussions results both from the compelling intellectual task of sorting out the multiple dimensions of cultural pluralism and from the transformative power of new subjects of study as students and faculty members engage them.

This engagement with questions of cultural multiplicity by institutions participating in the Cultural Legacies project is part of a larger trend in higher education. In a special issue of *Change* on multiculturalism and the curriculum, the Carnegie Foundation for the Advancement of Teaching reports that the curriculum of American colleges and universities is becoming increasingly diverse in response to the changing needs of society and the changing boundaries of scholarship.[5] The foundation's data show that between 1970 and 1985, the percentage of four-year colleges and universities with general-education requirements for at least one course in international/global education increased from 4.5 to 14.6 percent; in third world studies from 2.9 to 7.9 percent; and in women's studies from zero to 1.6 percent. Simultaneously, required courses in the history of Western civilization rose from 43.1 to 48.5 percent. By 1990, 53 percent of four-year colleges and universities required students to take a course in Western civilization, 46 percent in world civilizations, and 20 percent in racial/ethnic content. In an article in the same issue, Arthur Levine and Jeannette Cureton report that more than one-third of all colleges and universities now have a multicultural general-education requirement; at least a third offer course work in ethnic and gender studies; and more than one half have introduced multiculturalism into their departmental course offerings.[6] Jerry Gaff, in his survey of trends in general-education reform in *New Life for the College Curriculum*, found that global affairs and cultural diversity were the two trends campus leaders thought would most influence curricular change at their own institutions in the 1990s.[7]

Previous efforts to incorporate cultural pluralism in general-education curricula have followed two models:

- *requiring specialized courses from new interdisciplinary fields*: international studies, regional studies, American ethnic studies, third world studies, and women's studies

- *integrating theory, content, and pedagogy from these fields into courses across the curriculum.*

The first model, an additive one, has contributed to the ongoing development of new scholarship and scholarly fields that focus on the traditions, cultures, and histories of groups that had been marginalized. The existence of this base of scholarship provides an indispensable foundation for attempts to address cultural pluralism in core programs.

The second model—incorporating the study of cultural multiplicity across the curriculum—brings the new scholarship from these fields into a central place in the academy. The "across-the-curriculum" initiatives of the past several decades—international studies, women's studies, ethnic studies—have contributed both faculty development models and topical and thematic approaches for incorporating new content into the curriculum.[8] On campuses that choose this model, faculty members designing courses for general education are rethinking older paradigms for the study of civilizations and cultures and exploring ways to connect the values and experiences of disparate human societies across time and place. Neither of these models, however, creates a common framework for exploring cultural pluralism for all students.

The choices that present themselves to core curriculum planners who are thinking about culture, cultural legacies, and cultural relations are rendered more difficult by lack of clarity in national and campus discussions about multiculturalism. The term "multicultural" often is used to refer simultaneously to the study of African, Asian, Middle Eastern, Latin American, and other "world" cultures *and* to the study of "minority" cultures within the United States. (Until recently, the term referred primarily to the study of U.S. populations of color.) Some faculty members believe that exposure to any other country's culture, history, or language is sufficient to provide students with multicultural understanding; others insist that students must learn to analyze cultural relations in terms of power— that is, when and why difference means dominance of one culture over another.

These conceptual confusions about multiculturalism may manifest themselves in the design of curricular requirements. Disparate courses often are added to a "multicultural" menu when political compromises rather than student learning goals dictate curricular choices. In forging a "diversity" or multicultural distribution requirement, for example, faculty members may combine distinct content areas—lumping together all "otherness"—by requiring students to take a course on minority groups in the United States *or* a course on women *or* a course on non-Western culture *or* a foreign language. Students hardly learn what they need to know about U.S. populations of color by taking a course about a "non-Western" civilization in its golden age or by studying Russian. A course on Chinese philosophy has educational purposes that are quite different from a course on Native American women, and both differ fundamentally from a course on racism, sexism, anti-Semitism, homophobia, and other forms of prejudice and discrimination. Any or all of these courses may provide valuable learning experiences for students on a particular campus, but they attend to very different learning goals.

STUDENT LEARNING GOALS AND CONTENT CHOICES

Core curriculum planners in the Cultural Legacies project found it useful to begin limiting choices by thinking about their students and defining goals for student learning in terms appropriate to particular institutional contexts and missions. Thus, in embarking on the core program at Fairleigh Dickinson University, says Leonard Grob, core director and professor of philosophy, "we asked ourselves about the content, values, intellectual objectives and competencies we wished to foster in students."[9] Goals for the study of cultural legacies in these core humanities programs include:

- To help us overcome provinciality and transcend our own narrow sphere of experience (Earlham College)

- To foster a global perspective (Fairleigh Dickinson University)

- To encourage students to develop a broad international perspective on historical and cultural developments as a background for understanding the contemporary world (Washington State University)

- To develop in students the ability to "read" a culture through its cultural expressions; to develop in students the ability to see relationships, contrasts, parallels, commonalities and interactions among various cultures (LeMoyne-Owen College)

- To foster an appreciation of the diversity of knowledge traditions within the contemporary world (Carthage College)

- To increase students' sensitivity to issues of race, class, and gender (George Mason University)

- To consider ways various social groups within a given society participate in the culture of their society (Tufts University)

- To provide concepts and tools for understanding the social realities and problems in this moment in history (University of Oklahoma)

- To evaluate how men and women of diverse origins have interacted to produce rich cultures in the modern world (Hampton University)

- To help students identify, explore and evaluate concrete examples of their own cultural heritage and elucidate links between this heritage and other times and places (University of Wyoming)

While this list scarcely exhausts the range of potential goals, it calls attention to the importance of establishing purposes *before* designing curricula. Having an agreed-upon set of goals helps give direction when making choices about subject matter for courses.

Faculty members' sense of place sometimes fruitfully influenced their curricular choices. In designing core programs, it appears to make a difference whether you are in Pullman, Fairbanks, Los Angeles, Laramie, Memphis, or New York City, as these program rationales demonstrate:

> Washington State faces the Pacific and Asia.... [A] glance at [Washington State University's] student body makes it apparent that our students' relevant past is not just the past of Europe or the Mediterranean. Africa, Asia, the Pacific Islands, and ancient North America form part of our local heritage. And the fact of our single global economy, our single global political system of nation states, wars, and alliances, is but one of many considerations which make a global perspective in the curriculum desirable.

> Alaska is equidistant from the powerful forces of change in the modern world emerging from Asia and Europe.... Alaska lies 60 miles from the Soviet Union, and since the Cold War has had a large military population...nearly 11 percent of [University of Alaska–Fairbanks] students are Natives from rural regions throughout the state.... The stories of this culturally different population are used as a resource in the curriculum to enhance the experiences of all students while enhancing Native self-esteem.

> UCLA's entering freshmen classes are more than 60 percent ethnic majority, representing a confluence of Chicano/Latino, Asian Pacific, African American, and Native American heritages, as well as a burgeoning international population that enables us to re-situate Euro-American traditions within a new interdependent global world order. As Zena Pearlstone has written, "People from more that 140 countries today make their home in Los Angeles.... Children in the Los Angeles school system speak more than 90 different native languages."

> Eighty percent of [the University of Wyoming's] 10,000 undergraduates come from Wyoming and a majority of the remainder hail from neighboring states. Only nine Wyoming towns have more than 10,000 inhabitants and none has more than 50,000.... To serve the needs of students whose ethnic and cultural backgrounds are comparatively homogeneous, whose love of the state is often intense and sometimes defensive, and who will spend much of their lives, many reluctantly, in very different cultural and geographical settings, we felt it essential to begin with what is most familiar then work outward by

analogy and then by contrast…. To see Wyoming and the region as a crossroads, a place where time, space, and peoples intersect, is to change the metaphor of a bastion or a backwater which descriptions of the area might suggest.

LeMoyne-Owen [College] serves an African American commuter population of economically disadvantaged students from the public school system of Memphis, Tennessee and surrounding Mid-South region, large numbers of whom are first generation students. As at-risk commuter students from a southern city which is not ethnically diverse, many of them are provincial in their exposure, and limited in their cultural interaction.

Better understanding of the values and perspectives of other cultures and their histories is particularly relevant to Queens College [of the City University of New York] at a time when 44 percent of its 17,500 undergraduate students are immigrants or children of immigrants.

As these illustrations of institutional, student, and cultural diversity indicate, there can no longer exist a single paradigm—such as the traditional Western civilization course—that will suffice as core study about cultural legacies. The choices that present themselves to core curriculum planners searching for an organizing principle are virtually limitless: which societies to feature; how to study them; which themes, periods of time, texts, and authors to include.

PRAXIS

Typically, decisions about engaging cultural pluralism translate into discussions about the balance between "West" and "world" in new programs and how to frame "the West" within larger global perspectives. Engaging multiple cultural traditions with powerful and cohesive stories, but with unequal standing in traditional curricula, in the core of the undergraduate curriculum is daunting. Institutions in AAC's project came up with different models, all of which are still evolving.

West/World. Course designs represent a continuum of responses to possible emphases within and across cultural traditions:
- teaching Western civilization as the fundamental base for all cultural study
- teaching Western civilization centrally while consciously exploring the critical traditions within it and purposefully comparing it to other cultural traditions

- teaching Western civilization as one tradition to be studied among many.

Several institutions in the project had long-standing Western civilization courses; others were creating core programs with a Western emphasis when issues of cultural pluralism came to the fore and challenged earlier models for representing the West. The former case seemed to present the most difficulty for reform, given the close ties that established courses had to traditional departments, to assumptions about students' intellectual heritage, and to the identities and expertise of faculty members.

Faculty members on different campuses wrestled with the question of emphases and adopted very different solutions to the issue of balancing the study of cultural traditions. After heated debate, faculty members at Columbia College of Columbia University, for example, decided to sustain the Western focus of their Contemporary Civilization program (the oldest of the programs among the resource institutions in the Cultural Legacies project, dating back to 1918). Following a 1988 review of the curriculum, they reaffirmed the Western tradition as a distinctive set of paradigms fundamental to liberal education, as well as the importance of engaging students as both inheritors and makers of that tradition. However, the Columbia College faculty did reduce the Western studies requirement from two years to one in order to institute an Extended Core in 1989. The Extended Core includes two one-semester interdisciplinary courses: one in a major foreign culture, selected from a list, and the other in either still another major culture or a set of major issues of our times. Faculty members are beginning to plan integrated courses that meet the Extended Core requirement. For example, one group has developed a course entitled "Social Hierarchies."

In 1985, the University of Kansas (KU)—another resource institution for the project—reaffirmed the central place of Western civilization in its core but added one course on a non-Western culture as part of students' distribution requirements. The "Statement of Purpose for the Western Civilization Program" reads:

The Western Civilization Program, established as the Second World War ended in 1945, is expressive of the... institutional commitment to fostering rational inquiry into and constructive criticism of Western ideals and values. As such, Western Civilization is not a study of all human civilizations. The liberal arts and sciences general education requirement of undergraduate study in Asian, African, and other non-Western cultures is strongly endorsed by our program and should be pursued under the guidance of academic specialists in those areas.

The first semester of KU's Western Civilization Program explores the roots of Western civilization in ancient Mesopotamia and Egypt, Israel, and Greece; examines Roman civilization, early Christianity, and medieval Europe; and concludes with the Renaissance, the Reformation, and the scientific revolution. The second semester is organized thematically, beginning with the Enlightenment and study of social contracts and continuing through capitalism, industrialization, and the problem of social justice; science and its impact; the spiritual and moral crises of the modern era; and issues of power and domination. The textbook adopted for the course, *Patterns in Western Civilization*, incorporates some study of ethnicity, race, class, and gender.[10] Readings for the two semesters include traditional "great books" authors such as Sophocles and Plato, Augustine, Aquinas, Chaucer, Machiavelli, Luther, Galileo, Locke and Rousseau, Marx, Darwin, Nietzche, and Freud, together with writers such as Pizan, Wollstonecraft, Gilman, DuBois, Paz, Leopold, Beauvoir, Woolf, Wiesel, and King. The KU approach encourages reflection and analysis of Western traditions. Values encountered as part of cultures are critically assessed; histories of prejudice, such as anti-Semitism, are explored.

The College of St. Francis' two-semester freshman core course "Self, Society, and Nature," also primarily Western-based, adopts the perspective that the central quality of the Western tradition is its self-critical nature. One goal for this course is to have students come to see themselves as part of a nation, a culture, a race, and a gender. Similarly, at Western Washington University, the proposed three-quarter freshman core course relies almost exclusively on major Western writers such as Plato, Cicero, Luther, Marx, Austen, and Goethe. Yet the course planners write, "[W]estern culture is not monolithic or hermetically contained, but comprises a variety and succession of alternatives and antinomies emerging in relation to impulses arising within European experience and from outside it. The course aims to acquaint students with this variety and ambiguity within European culture."[11]

Many faculty members fear that if a core curriculum focuses centrally on Western traditions, students may receive an unintended message that only the West and its inheritances are sufficiently important to merit inclusion in a program of common study. A number of faculty teams in the project expressed the view that the decision to build an integrated core program around Western issues, leaving the rest of the world to a less-valued distribution requirement, ran counter to the goal of helping students grasp the interdependence of the world community. Given these concerns, the majority of the planning institutions have explored ways of creating deliberate curricular connections between the West and the world.

In its new core, Fairleigh Dickinson University substantially expands the Western tradition and connects it to world studies. In its four lower-division core courses—"Perspectives on the Individual," "The American Experience," "Cross-Cultural Perspectives," and "Global Issues"—attention to different cultures enters at the beginning. Geoffrey Weinman, vice president for academic affairs, describes the design process:

> We...recognized early on that the idea of the individual...was largely a Western conception, and that this course [Core I: Perspectives on the Individual] would therefore not adequately address the issue of multicultural perspectives, if by that we meant that the works chosen were to include voices from cultures throughout the world, especially the developing or third world. The issue of gender and race was one we would have to address....
>
> In Core II, we begin with an analysis of the sacred texts of the American "Western tradition": the Bill of Rights, the Declaration of Independence, the Gettysburg address, the Battle Hymn of the Republic, and King's "I Have a Dream" speech. As we read these works, we ask our students, who are "all men"? What is the basis of individual rights? Are we a religious people? What is the American dream and who is included in it?...
>
> Having focused on the Western tradition in Core I and examined aspects of its impact on the American experience in Core II, we are ready in the third course to examine Cross-Cultural Perspectives by exploring patterns of the traditional cultures of Nigeria, Mexico, India, and China and the ways in which our Western ideas relate to them. We also try to get students to consider the culture they are reading and writing about in terms of one or more of the books they have read in the first two Core courses....
>
> Finally, in Core IV, Global Issues, we look beyond the limits or boundaries of a culture and society to address some of those issues that touch us all: issues such as AIDS, nuclear warfare, and environmental pollution.[12]

Within these four courses, students examine Western perspectives and use them to explore a host of issues that, in the past, were seldom explored in traditional Western civilization courses.

FAIRLEIGH DICKINSON UNIVERSITY
SELECTED READINGS

CORE I **Perspectives on the Individual**
Margaret Atwood, *The Handmaid's Tale*
Gilgamesh
Plato, *Euthyphro, Apology* and *Crito*
Pico Della Mirandola, "Oration on the Dignity of Man"
Shakespeare, *Sonnets*
William Wordsworth, "Tintern Abbey" and "Ode: Intimations
   of Immortality from Recollections of Early Childhood"
Sigmund Freud, *Civilization and Its Discontents*
Franz Kafka, "The Metamorphosis"
Tillie Olsen, *Tell Me a Riddle*
The Autobiography of Malcolm X
Elie Wiesel, *Night*

CORE II **The American Experience: The Quest for Freedom**
Herbert McCloskey and John Zaller, *The American Ethos*
The Declaration of Independence
The United States Bill of Rights
"The Seneca Falls Declaration of Sentiments"
Sojourner Truth, "Ain't I a Woman"
Benjamin Franklin, *The Autobiography and Other Writings*
Narrative of the Life of Frederick Douglass
Joanna L. Stratton, *Pioneer Women*
Henry David Thoreau, *Walden* and *Civil Disobedience*
Upton Sinclair, *The Jungle*
Joan and Robert K. Morrison, *From Camelot to Kent State*
Selected poems by Anne Sexton, Ray Young Bear, Julia Ward
   Howe, Dudley Randall, Askia Muhammad Touré, Langston Hughes
Roe v. Wade; Webster v. Reproductive Health Services
Catherine MacKinnon, "The Sexual Politics of the First Amendment"

CORE III **Cross-Cultural Perspectives**
Chinua Achebe, *Things Fall Apart*
Buchi Emecheta, *The Joys of Motherhood*
The Bhagavad-Gita: Krishna's Counsel in Times of War
Zhang Xinxin and Sang Ye, *Chinese Lives:*
   An Oral History of Modern China
Gregorio Lopez y Fuentes, *El Indio*
Oscar Lewis, *Five Families: Mexican Case Studies in the*
   Culture of Poverty

CORE IV **Global Issues**
Albert Camus, *The Plague*
AIDS and the Third World
John Hersey, *Hiroshima*
Richard Lo Pinto, *Pollution*
Arthur Miller, adaptation of Henrik Ibsen's *An Enemy of the People*
Richard Morris, *Dismantling the Universe*
Annie Dillard, *Pilgrim at Tinker Creek*
Martin Buber, *I and Thou*

In the University of Richmond's core course, "Exploring Human Experience" (see pages 20–21), most of the texts are Western, but they are purposefully compared with texts from other cultures. Texts from East Asia were introduced in the first year of a three-year pilot phase (1991–92) and texts from Africa in the second year (1992–93). Texts from the Middle East will be added in the final year.

In the core program at Mount St. Mary's College (Md.), first-year students take a year-long course in Western history paired with a contemporaneous course in literature or the arts. Beginning in 1990–91, these paired courses introduced "windows" on non-European texts or political developments so that, for example, students consider Islam as they read the *Song of Roland* and Chinua Achebe's *Things Fall Apart* as they study the colonization of Africa.

Hampton University's "Humanities 201–202: Enduring Human Values and Cultural Connections" is a two-semester interdisciplinary course that introduces students to Western and non-Western cultural legacies through the study of works of art, literature, and music from antiquity to the present. The focus is on exploring cultural contact and collision: the impact of the West on other cultures and other cultures on the West. Multiplicity is the organizing principle; in the first term, for example, students analyze the role of epics in forming human values by reading *The Odyssey, The Iliad, Gilgamesh,* and *Sundiata.*

The four sequential Heritage Studies seminars at Carthage College approach "heritage" as ideas, values, and assumptions generated through complex transactions over time among human beings within and across communities. The first course in the sequence challenges students to reflect on their own education in the West. Through the study of texts including Shakespeare's *Tempest,* Shelley's *Frankenstein,* and Beethoven's Ninth Symphony, students confront questions about the nature and consequences of personal and cultural knowledge: How can we best discover, construct, and transmit what we most need to know? How—for better or worse—can knowledge transform individuals and societies? Questions of liberty, justice, and equality also are addressed. In Heritage II, students study some of the ways Western experience is redefined and re-imagined through encounters between European and African cultures. Nineteenth-century colonialism is approached from two contrasting perspectives: Joseph Conrad's *Heart of Darkness* and Chinua Achebe's *Things Fall Apart.* Juxtaposing these two texts encourages students to engage powerful questions about beauty, goodness, and truth.

The third Heritage seminar introduces another culture—currently Japanese culture—and engages questions of individuality and community, tradition and innovation, rationality and spirituality, and war and peace. In the final Heritage seminar, students approach U.S. culture through questions of individuality and community, difference and mutuality, memory and change. Representative texts include Richard Rodriguez's *Hunger of Memory*, Zora Neale Hurston's *Their Eyes Were Watching God*, Tim O'Brien's *The Things They Carried*, and Louise Erdrich's *Love Medicine*.

World studies. While most of the institutions in the Cultural Legacies project made the West a primary and distinctive axis for their core programs, several institutions organized their programs as world studies. These world studies programs include units on Western history and culture but embed them in larger narratives that show the West as part of a larger world community. Those who make the world rather than the West the organizing framework for core courses argue that this approach best responds to the global challenges confronting today's students, who must come to see themselves and their nation as linked to others economically, ecologically, and politically.

Within the Cultural Legacies project, there are two fundamental approaches to world studies programs. In the "intensive study" model, faculty members organize the material through a combination of case studies and themes used to examine generative periods in selected world cultures. In the "historical/developmental" model, core planners adopt a historical framework, exploring changes and pivotal moments in major world civilizations over time.

The first approach is similar to that of Western civilization courses that focus in some depth on specific periods in Western European history, such as the High Middle Ages or seventeenth-century England. The predilection for theme as an organizing principle stems from many impulses: the desire to connect texts and topics from different cultures that may not necessarily be contemporary; to explore fundamental dimensions of human experience such as faith, virtue, memory; to introduce interdisciplinary or multidisciplinary perspectives; or to incorporate the study of race, class, gender, and ethnicity.

The University of Denver's "Civilizations Compared" provides one example of using themes to connect disparate cultures and historic moments. This year-long, three-quarter sequence focuses on ideas of excellence and virtue in major world civilizations. In the fall quarter, these themes are explored in relation to the literature, religion, and social tradi-

UNIVERSITY OF RICHMOND
INTERDISCIPLINARY CORE COURSE 101–102, 1992–93
ISSUES IN HUMAN EXPERIENCE

ORDER AND CHANGE

Order and *change* are related dimensions of the human experience that have engaged the attention of thinkers in virtually all cultures and periods of history. Over the course of the year we will be studying texts that have raised a variety of questions about the ways in which our life and world are structured and the ways in which those structures are transformed. Our purpose will not be the limited one of answering our own personal questions about these matters, but rather the broader purpose of understanding how very differently questions about order and change (or about other dimensions of human experience) can be asked and addressed by thinkers responding to widely different situations and interests.

Fall 1992

INTRODUCTION

8/26–28	Preliminaries
8/31–9/4	Overview: Forster, *A Passage to India* (We begin our investigation of order and change with a text in which the problem is the very relationship between the two, and in which that relationship is explored from several different cultural perspectives. In these ways, Forster's novel introduces us both to themes and to methods that will occupy us throughout the course.)

ORDER

MORAL ORDER. What is justice and what does it require of us? How are guilt and punishment related? How do our ideas of right and wrong shape our experience of the world? What obligations do they entail? What can we do when these obligations are in conflict?

9/7–11	Soyinka, *Death and the King's Horseman*
9/14–18	*Genesis*
9/21–25	New Testament (Gospel of Matthew and/or John)
9/28–10/2	Dante, *Inferno*
10/5–9	Nietzsche, *On the Genealogy of Morals*

SOCIAL ORDER. How is society organized? What are the proper functions and limits of power? What can be done when power fails in its proper functions or exceeds its proper limits? What are the benefits and costs of civilization?

10/12–16	*Sundiata*
10/21–23	*Mencius*
10/26–30	Rousseau, *Discourse on the Origins of Inequality*
11/2–6	Freud, *Civilization and Its Discontents*

FAMILIAR ORDER. How are our lives shaped by the claims of family, home, sexual relations and friendship? What are the benefits and costs of the order that these establish in our lives? How do these claims interact with those of the moral and social order?

11/9–13   Shostak, *Nisa*
11/16–24   Homer, *The Odyssey*
11/30–12/4 Chikamatsu, *Love Suicides at Amijima*
12/7–8   Conclusion: The problem of order

Spring 1993

CHANGE

SELF-DISCOVERY AND CHANGE. How fixed is one's self? How susceptible of change? How can we know our inner nature? How is it affected by forces outside us? How can we control or change it?

1/6–8   Woolf, *A Room of One's Own*
1/11–15   Augustine, *Confessions*
1/18–22   Shakespeare, *King Lear*
1/25–29   Wordsworth, *The Prelude*

EDUCATION AND CHANGE. How do we acquire and construct knowledge? How are we changed by that process? What knowledge is worth pursuing? Which kinds of knowledge are we capable of pursuing and which must elude us? How is knowledge related to power and control?

2/1–5   Plato, *Meno* and *Apology*
2/8–12   *Chuang Tzu*
2/15–19   Dangarembga, *Nervous Conditions*
2/22–26   Sōseki, *Kokoro*

SOCIAL CHANGE AND POLITICAL CHANGE. How should society be changed? What instruments are available for changing it? What are the benefits and costs of their use? Can harmful social change be avoided or controlled?

3/1–5   Achebe, *Things Fall Apart*
3/15–19   Locke, *Second Treatise of Government; Declaration of the Rights of Man and Citizen*; Olympe de Gouges, *Declaration of the Rights of Women; Declaration of Independence*
3/22–26   Marx and Engels, *Communist Manifesto* and other writings
3/29–4/2 Lao She, *Rickshaw*
4/5–9   Fanon, *Wretched of the Earth*
4/12–16   DeLillo, *White Noise*
4/19–20   Conclusion: The problem of change

tions of classical China and Greece. In the winter quarter, students study morality and ideals in Judaism, Islam, and Christianity. In the spring quarter, the course again returns to China, now comparing its revolutionary tradition with American and French revolutionary aspirations. By exploring unifying themes across time and culture, students gain a perspective on their own tradition and a way to grasp core issues within complex traditions.

Students at Tufts University choose from among three two-semester, thematically organized World Civilizations sequences: "A Sense of Place," "Time and Calendars," and "Memory and Identity in World Cultures." Each theme serves as a statement about human experience and as a structuring device to help students understand the material. Students explore and elaborate these themes through the study of at least three cultures. The themes allow cross-cultural analysis and a representative sampling of diverse human cultures.

All of the humanities core courses at Brandeis University are organized around themes such as human nature, law and morality, beauty, language and persuasion, individual responsibility, causality, and mortality. Traditionally, these themes have been developed through Western texts; now, as part of an attempt to bring multiple voices into its program, Brandeis faculty members select from a wider range of traditions (see pages 24–25). Under a Ford Foundation faculty-development grant, twenty-one courses have been revised to include African and African American materials.

In two of the world cultures courses developed through the Cultural Legacies project, the organizing principle is the study of culture itself. The University of Oklahoma has piloted several sections of a proposed core course, "World Cultures and Traditions," that helps first-year students develop analytic frameworks for studying the nature of culture and cultural change. The first semester is organized synchronically, with several common themes and instructor-specific emphases. A "universal" aspect of human experience—for example, the passage from childhood to adulthood, or illness and death—anchors discussion of each theme or topic. The second semester is diachronic, examining the dynamics of cultural conflict and cultural change. Faculty members teaching this course have agreed that each cultural topic will be illustrated by texts from at least three different world cultures. They are convinced that this approach avoids overly simplistic comparisons and helps students begin to grasp the complexity and diversity of human societies.

Carnegie Mellon University is piloting a two-semester course that

TUFTS UNIVERSITY
WORLD CIVILIZATIONS 001

A SENSE OF PLACE: CULTURAL CONSTRUCTIONS OF PLACE

INTRO: THE ORIGINS OF PLACE: MYTHS, MEANING, AND CONTEXT
1. Creation of the World: Man and Woman's Place
2. The Loss of Paradise: Labor and Disease
3. Competition for Resources: City, Village, Pasture, Forest
Literary Texts: *Gilgamesh*, Genesis, Cherokee myths
Architectural Text: Ziggurat at Ur

UNIT I: THE CLASSICAL MEDITERRANEAN
4. Geography of the Mediterranean World: Land and Sea
5. The Impact of Greek Maritime Technology
6. From Greek City-state to Roman Empire
7. The Classical Imprint: Technology and Architecture
8. The Classical Imprint: The World of Ideas
Literary Texts: Aristotle, Archimedes
Architectural Texts: Parthenon, Ephesus, Pantheon

UNIT II: CHINA'S EMPIRE: THE MIDDLE KINGDOM
9. Geography of Eastern Eurasia: Agriculture and Pastoralism
10. China and the Middle Kingdom
11. Confucian World View and Nomadic World View
12. The Great Wall and the Tribute System
Literary Texts: Confucius, Mencius, Turkic inscriptions
Architectural Texts: Imperial Palace at Changan

UNIT III: ISLAM AND THE MIDDLE EAST
13. Arabia's Place in the Late Classical World
14. The Arab Appropriation of Classical Cultures
15. The Preservation of Arab Identity: The Construction of the
Bedouin Ideal
16. The Islamic Imprint: Architecture and Technology
17. The Islamic Imprint: The World of Ideas
Literary Texts: Pre-Islamic odes, Hadith
Architectural Texts: Great Mosque at Damascus, city plan of Baghdad

UNIT IV: WEST AFRICA: THE INTEGRATION OF SAVANNAH AND
FOREST
18. Geography, Expansion of Agriculture, and Derived Savannah
19. The West African Imperial System: Medieval Ghana and Mali
20. The Sudanic Mosque: West African Islam
21. Local and Imperial Values in *The Epic of Sundiata*
Literary Text: *The Epic of Sundiata*
Architectural Texts: Mosque at Jenne, Kama-blon at Kangaba

UNIT V: THE WESTERN HEMISPHERE: REGIONAL INTEGRATION
BEFORE 1492
22. Incas: Linkages within the Andean Ecosystem
23. Anasazi: Southwestern Road Networks
24. Mississippians: Riverine Systems
25. Technology and Structures of the Western Hemisphere
Literary Texts: Native American legend
Architectural Texts: Chaco Canyon ruins, the kiva

BRANDEIS UNIVERSITY

HUM1 29a: Imagining How We Are I
(Luis Yglesias, Fall 1991; enrollment 100)

The great texts of antiquity present us with images of how we are and what the world we must act in is like, images with which we may want to argue but which are indispensable to modern consciousness. Greece, Rome and the Near East have bequeathed us a complex and perhaps contradictory tradition contained in a handful of wondrous tales which this course will examine in terms of the metaphysics they either generate or which appear to support them. But do the stories of Homer and Sophocles, Plato and the Old and New Testaments tell us all that antiquity can teach us about what is grave and constant in human affairs? Brief selections from Hindu, Taoist, and Buddhist texts will also be read throughout the term in order to provide ample opportunities for lively discussions on this issue.

Texts: Homer, *The Iliad, The Odyssey*; Sophocles, *Oedipus Rex, Oedipus at Colonus*; Heraclitus; Socrates/Plato, *Apology*; *Enuma Elish*; *Gilgamesh*; Genesis, Exodus; Apuleius, *Golden Ass*; Gospel according to Matthew; *Bhagavad Gita*; *Upanishads*; Lao Tzu, *Chuang Tzu*, selected Buddhist texts

HUM2 48b: Imagining How We Are II
(Luis Yglesias, Spring 1992; enrollment 100)

Shakespeare's *Tempest* provides us with this semester's theme as we explore the impact of "Brave New Worlds" on the old world sense of how we are and what the world we must act in is like. We begin with the first modern East-West opposition as established in *Roland* which denies any value to the world of Islam. Then, after a corrective excursus into that enormously sophisticated world, we return to Gottfried's *Tristan*, a heterodox text that challenges Christianity in the name of passion and which proposes a view of reality profoundly influenced by Islam. Rojas' *Celestina*, our next text, tells a love story which takes place in a world secularized as a result of Spain's effort to suppress both Judaism and Islam. A fascinating result is the first self-conscious presentation of class conflict, which is another variation in our theme. With *The Tempest* we begin a series of journeys (the Hsi-yu-Chi, *Huckleberry Finn, Kim*) that variously attempt to come to terms with a cultural other which we now can see is a fundamental task of our own period. Next, Tanizaki's classic *Some Prefer Nettles*, supported by selections from traditional Japanese literature, traces the Westernized protagonist's rejection of European values in terms that contrast dramatically with America's romance with Japan as recorded in Kerouac's *The Dharma Bums*. We end with a novel by Zora Neale Hurston that restates our theme in terms of gender and race conflict.

Texts: *Song of Roland*; Gottfried, *Tristan*; Rojas, *Celestina*; Shakespeare, *The Tempest*; *Hsi-yü Chi, Monkey*; Twain, *Huckleberry Finn*; Kipling, *Kim*; Tanizaki, *Some Prefer Nettles*; Kerouac, *The Dharma Bums*; Zora Neale Hurston, *Their Eyes Were Watching God*

HUM2 52b: Not for the Fainthearted
(Erica Harth, Spring 1992; enrollment 25)
Who's human in the humanities? Women? People of color? The poor?
What the Western tradition has had to say about human nature raises
these questions. The very notion of the "humanities" is built on the
assumption that there exists a permanent human nature in which we all
share and which is intelligible to everyone. But if I am a slaveholder, do I
view my slave as a fully human being? How did slaves partake of human
nature as it is conceptualized in the humanities? Through our readings, we
will pose "human nature" as a problem: To what extent do the readings
present it as a given—inborn, biological, or physiological—or as socially
and culturally constructed? During the successive social transformations of
the past four hundred years, ideas about the constitutive features of
humanity, such as masculinity, femininity, sexuality, and power, have
undergone striking change. At key historical moments—the transition
from an agricultural, precapitalist society to industrial capitalism, and,
more recently, the transition to the post-industrial era—Western society
has had to rethink the relation of nature and culture, the social meaning
and explanatory value of these concepts. We will be looking for the
shifting ground of the nature/culture debate as we analyze the treatment of
sex, class, and race in imaginative literature and critical thought. This
course is not for the fainthearted: it may make you uncomfortable!

Texts: Freud, *Civilization and Its Discontents*; Montaigne, *Essays*;
Shakespeare, *The Tempest*; Rousseau, *Discourse on Inequality*; Césaire, *A
Tempest*; Dickens, *Hard Times*; Marx and Engels, *The Communist Manifesto*;
Jacobs, *Incidents in the Life of a Slave Girl, Written by Herself*; Gilman, "The
Yellow Wallpaper"; Morrison, *Sula*

takes a similar approach. Proposed as part of a more comprehensive general-education reform, "World Cultures/Cultural Studies" begins in fall 1992 with a half-semester introduction to cultural studies. Students then elect one of two half-semester courses: either a course in Asian-American cultures or one focusing on "professional cultures."

Massachusetts Bay Community College offers an example of a case-study approach. In a new, team-taught course, "World Traditions: Yesterday and Today," faculty members present three case studies drawn from African, Middle Eastern, and United States cultural history. The cases are linked by exploration of themes such as values and family structures. At the same time, each case stands on its own as a unit that explores a particular time and place. The United States unit, for example, addresses the nineteenth century and looks at both free and enslaved families.

In the second model for framing world studies, course planners take a historical or developmental approach, organizing the subject matter to trace the emergence of an interdependent world community. This model allows more attention to the dynamics of change and to interrelationships among different societies; it is less oriented to multiple meanings within particular societies at particular moments in time.

Washington State University, for example, requires all students to take a two-semester course, "World Civilizations," that examines historically the development of Eastern and Western civilizations, ancient and modern. The course is organized chronologically and seeks a balance between examining the particular parts of the world and exploring comparisons and exchanges across different parts of the world.

At LeMoyne-Owen College, students begin by examining the African and African American heritage in a year-long interdisciplinary course, historical in approach; the course explores African roots, diaspora, and the varied experiences of Africans in the western hemisphere. In their sophomore year, students embark on a three-semester interdisciplinary course, "Human Heritage," which uses historical inquiry and concepts of world view and cultural legacy to elucidate major civilizations across time and place, beginning with Egypt and Mesopotamia.

Queens College of the City University of New York has developed one of the most ambitious programs in world studies: a four-semester sequence that combines the study of particular societies with a world systems approach. In an internal planning document, one of the faculty planners described the program's goals:

[All four courses ask:] What is the nature of the world system that many feel has emerged in modern times, and to what extent can we construct a historical narrative of its development from the ancient world to the present day? Second, how can we train ourselves to encounter a culture—ancient or modern—that is different in its history and conceptions of the world from our own, so that we can understand both its institutions and its religions, intellectual and artistic traditions? How can we, in short, appreciate both patterns of interconnectedness in world history and also the extreme particularity and diversity of specific cultures?...

Throughout all the courses, the world will be the unit of analysis within which material is studied. Rather than treating works from different cultures in isolation or simply as examples of variety, works shall be studied in relation to each other, each offering a commentary on the others.... Pedagogically, a chief goal of the program would be to bring students to awareness simultaneously of how their historical and cultural positions are connected to and different from those studied throughout world history—how, for each student, consciousness of difference is also consciousness of relationship.

In the first semester, "Interpreting the World," Queens College students—themselves often from families recently arrived in the United States—study examples of migrations and cross-cultural encounters. The objective is to help students develop an understanding of different strategies, humanistic and social scientific, for understanding cultural transactions and interactions. In the second semester, the course turns to the ancient world, focusing in particular on concepts of cosmos and state from pre-state societies to the rise of empires. The third course—which spans the period from the "age of exploration" to 1945—emphasizes intercultural contacts among civilizations: for example, Mexico and the arrival of Spanish colonizers. The fourth course explores the development since 1945 of an increasingly interactive world community as seen from different historical, ideological, and cultural positions and different disciplinary perspectives. Throughout all four courses, the emphasis is on joining interpretive frameworks from original sources, from scholarship in the humanities and social sciences, and from students' own experiences.

Teaching texts. Cutting across both content models for cultural legacies courses—West/world and world studies—is a predominant concern for teaching students to read rich texts and engage powerful themes. Brandeis' Core director, Karen Klein, chooses for her core course

"Survival" narrative texts that confront the human dilemma of mortality
by retelling traumatic events of great magnitude for individuals and societies and that illustrate the personal and communal meanings of life in the
face of death. The use of subthemes is important. In the first course seg-
ment—which includes Homer's *Odyssey*, the book of *Exodus*, and Toni
Morrison's *Beloved*, for example—the theme of journey lends itself to subthemes of self-definition, the individual and the community, relation to
place, homecoming, and the opposition of bondage and freedom. In other
segments of the course, students explore their place in the scheme of things
and the meaning and importance of human love and connections. Klein
also juxtaposes *The Iliad* with Tim O'Brien's "How to Tell a War Story" to
illustrate generational, class, and political conflict along with themes of
moral choice, loyalty, and betrayal. Students in the course are conscious of
this strategy and appreciate the comparison of human responses to moral
dilemmas and choices then and now.

Some courses juxtapose art with literary texts and teach students
how to "read" both. Barbara Frankle, professor of history and associate dean
of the faculty for CORE curriculum and faculty development at LeMoyne-
Owen College, opens her "Human Heritage" course by having students
examine art and writings from traditional African and Asian cultures: an
eighth-century Chinese tomb ornament representing a saddled camel; a
West African headdress with antelopes; a tenth-century Chinese ink
painting of a mountain and valley entitled "Festival of the Rain"; Ashanti
proverbs; a passage on ethics and politics from Confucius; a tenth-century
neo-Confucian poem, "Song of Happiness"; and other cultural artifacts.
Students learn about the world view of these cultures by examining these
different "texts." In discussing these manifestations of cultural world views,
Frankle discourages students from making judgments about the relative
worth of the texts or elaborate comparisons among them. Students concentrate on analyzing the texts and drawing hypotheses that they can test in
more detail as the course proceeds.

In such approaches, students are being introduced to a new way of
seeing and evaluating commonality and relationship across cultures. Tamar
March, vice president for academic affairs at New England College, wrote
to one faculty member in the project about this approach:

> The respect with which you treated all the texts on the syllabus was
> striking. It was genuine, it privileged no culture over another, and
> thereby implicitly demonstrated that no matter what point on the
> globe one happens to be, there is universality in the stories we tell

each other across generations, across continents, stories that express
our deepest humanity. That is altogether different from learning, as I
did as a child, that Racine and Moliere, that Shakespeare and
Dickens, are *classics* because they are universal. Your course provides
the experience, rather than the statement, of that universality.…
More than multi-cultural, this course is global…students coming out
of your course…will have an orientation to the world which will be
new and different from past generations of students.[13]

United States pluralism. Fewer institutions in the Cultural
Legacies project—about 25 percent of the total—include or propose a
required course on pluralism within the United States as part of the core. It
may be easier and less threatening to engage difference at a distance—
where it is expected and anticipated and where one has no permanent
responsibility as a citizen—than at home. Yet faculty planners at several
institutions expressed deep concern about student parochialism regarding
the multiplicity of cultural heritages within the United States and their
historic and contemporary interactions. They wanted their students to
develop a context for analyzing complex cultural issues such as those
embedded in the Clarence Thomas confirmation hearings, conflicts over
fishing rights and development on tribal lands, or Supreme Court rulings
on civil rights law. Students' lack of perspective on current events stems in
part from the U.S. educational system's perpetuation of the myth of the
melting pot and its denial of cultural conflict of any real import. Even
those students who have not been willing or able to "melt down" often
have not studied formally their own and other "minority" cultures and
their historical interactions.

We already have seen the central placement of the United States
in the core programs at Fairleigh Dickinson University and Carthage
College. At Samford University, the final two core courses in a six-course
sequence address "The American Experience," encompassing Latin
America and the United States and exploring the New World experience
as a fusion of Old World traditions and native cultures. These courses (still
under development) treat the influence of Europe, Africa, and Eastern
cultures upon the United States of today.

Goals for the Tennessee State University humanities core program
include heightening students' awareness of their relationship to three cultural legacies: the U.S. legacy of cultural diversity, an increasingly interrelated international culture, and a culture of liberally educated persons. The
first-year pilot core courses are linked U.S. history and English composition

courses with reading assignments exploring U.S. cultural groups. The text-book used in the composition courses, *American Mosaic: Multicultural Readings in Context*, presents a variety of materials—legal documents, historical scholarship, poetry, fiction, and nonfiction—that enable students to study ethnic groups in the United States from both an external and an internal perspective.

After taking a required year-long course in "World Civilizations," students at SUNY–Buffalo are required as sophomores to select a course under the "American Pluralism and the Search for Equality" requirement. Each of the courses that fulfill this requirement examines the multicultural, multi-ethnic nature of United States society. "Conceived to serve as a basis for informed discourse," the course description notes, "the intention behind the course [requirement] is to provide undergraduate students with an intellectual awareness of the causes and effects of structured inequalities and prejudicial exclusion in the United States and of the processes leading to a more equitable society." The objective is to help students locate United States social and cultural experiences in the larger context of a diverse yet interconnected world community.

Faculty planners at institutions that envisage including both world cultures and U.S. pluralism frequently debate the benefits for students of starting with the "Ancients" versus starting with contemporary issues. The year-long introductory core course, "Crossroads," at the University of Wyoming (see pages 32–33) begins with the present and uses the crossroads metaphor as an organizing principle for the course. Unit I, The Land, begins with the local Wyoming context and explores conflicts between Euro-American and Native American concepts and between environmentalists and multiple-use advocates' interpretations of land use. Unit II, The Hero, explores conceptions of heroes in contemporary United States culture, in the Western European heritage, and in non-Western traditions. Unit III, Urban and Rural Cultures, and Unit IV, Equality, also juxtapose texts from different times and cultures.

Race, class, gender, ethnicity. A few planning institutions in the Cultural Legacies project included as specific goals acquainting students with gender, race, class, ethnicity, and other constructed dimensions of human diversity. Some of these institutions had held faculty development workshops on incorporating ethnic studies and women's studies across the curriculum. Fairleigh Dickinson University, for example, was influenced by the curriculum transformation work of the New Jersey Project—the first statewide project to fund curriculum transformation (with support from the State

TENNESSEE STATE UNIVERSITY
ENGLISH 102U: FRESHMAN COMPOSITION
(DR. CLAYTON C. REEVE, SPRING 1991)

Textbooks for Special Sections on Cultural Legacies
Barbara Roche Rico and Sandra Mano, eds. *American Mosaic: Multicultural Readings in Context*. Houghton Mifflin Company.

Section 1. Chinese Immigrants: The Lure of the Gold Mountain
The Chinese Exclusion Act (1882)
Maxine Hong Kingston, "The Grandfather of the Sierra Nevada Mountains"
Betty Lee Sung, "The Pioneer Chinese"
"The Gold Mountain Poems"
Videotape on Maxine Hong Kingston

Section 2. Native Americans: Pride and Cultural Heritage
The Indian Removal Act (1830)
N. Scott Momaday, "January 26"
Kenneth Lincoln, "Old Like Hills, Like Stars"

Section 3. Chicanos: Negotiating Economic and Cultural Boundaries
The Treaty of Guadalupe Hidalgo (1848)
Jose Antonio Villarreal, "Pocho"
Pat Mora, "Illegal Alien Legal Alien"

Section 4. Puerto Ricans: The View from the Mainland
The Foraker Act (1900)
Piri Thomas, "Puerto Rican Paradise"
Juan Flores, "Puerto Rican Literature in the United States: Stages and Perspectives"

Section 5. Japanese Americans: The Internment Experience
Japanese Relocation Order (1942)
Monica Sone, "Pearl Harbor Echoes in Seattle"
Jeanne Wakatsuki Houston and James Houston, "Farewell to Manzanar"

Section 6. African Americans: The Migration North and the Harlem Renaissance
The Constitution of South Carolina (1895)
Alain Locke, "The New Negro"
Zora Neale Hurston, "Sweat"

Section 7. African Americans: The Struggle for Civil Rights
Brown v. Board of Education of Topeka (1954)
Martin Luther King, Jr., "Letter from Birmingham Jail"; "I Have a Dream"
Malcolm X, from *The Autobiography of Malcolm X*

UNIVERSITY OF WYOMING

UNIVERSITY STUDIES 1200
CROSSROADS: EXPLORING CULTURAL LEGACIES (3 hours)

Course Schedule and Outline
The course is divided into four units, each of which will be 3–4 weeks in length. It begins with Owen Wister's *The Virginian*, a popular turn-of-the-century novel set in Wyoming and written by an Easterner. Each subsequent unit begins with a discussion of the ways in which the novel presents specific perspectives relevant to the focus of the unit. A second source text, placed on reserve, will be the catalogue of the recent, controversial Smithsonian exhibit, "The West as America: Reinterpreting Images of the Frontier."

For each unit, each student will select a reading from a bibliography to be provided.

1. The Land (Weeks 1–4)
This unit explores relationships among the land and agriculture, the environment, nature, recreation, water, and wilderness. Much in this unit concerns conflict—for example, the conflicts of the Euro-American concept of land contrasted with American Indian land use, environmental groups' interpretations of land-use versus multiple-use advocates in the American West. The unit will also examine how American and other cultures make sense of these concepts.

  Owen Wister, *The Virginian*
  Wendell Berry, *The Unsettling of America*
  Joel Garreau, "The Empty Quarter," from *The Nine Nations of North America*
  Kamala Markandaya, *Nectar in a Sieve*
  Roderick Nash, from *Wilderness and the American Mind*
  Linda Hasselstrom, from *Windbreak*

2. The Hero (Weeks 5–8)
This unit explores the conceptions about heroes in the contemporary American civilization, in our Western European heritage, and in non-Western traditions. Who are the heroes? Why are they considered heroic? How do gender, race, and nationality influence our understanding of heroism? Why do we need heroes?

  Owen Wister, *The Virginian*
  Beowulf
  Mahatma Gandhi, *All Men are Brothers*
  R.W.B. Lewis, *The American Adam*
  Sophocles, *Antigone*

3. Urban and Rural Cultures (Weeks 9–11)
This unit explores the values, ideas, and opportunities associated with the differences between urban and rural cultures. A historical context for the development of modern cities will be provided.

  Owen Wister, *The Virginian*
  Joseph Cook, from *Diary and Letters of the Rev. Joseph W. Cook, Missionary to Cheyenne*
  Michel-Guillaume Jean de Crevecoeur, from *Letters from an American Farmer*
  Ngugi wa Thiongo, *A Grain of Wheat*

4. Equality (Weeks 12–16)

This unit focuses on equality with respect to race, class, and gender, examining questions of freedom, prejudice, and morality. Students will examine Wyoming as the Equality State, equality within the U.S., and equality in an international setting.

Owen Wister, *The Virginian*

Chief Washakie, selected viewpoints drawn from AHC archives

John Locke, from *Second Treatise on Government*

Thomas Hobbes, *Leviathan*

Christine de Pizan, *The Book of the City of Ladies*

Aristophanes, *Lysistrata*

Chinua Achebe, *Things Fall Apart*

Department of Higher Education). FDU's strategy was to integrate the study of gender, race, class, and ethnicity into core courses through selections of texts that elucidate these variables (see course readings, page 17).

Among the most sophisticated examples of core courses incorporating the study of multiple variables of human identity are the SUNY–Buffalo "American Pluralism" courses mentioned above. Few courses outside of ethnic studies and women's studies have expectations for in-depth analysis of gender, race, class, ethnicity, and religion, and their intersections in both individual and group identity, as explicit as those in the "Goals and Standards" for these courses. The courses developed for the core are taught by many different faculty members, including ethnic studies and women's studies specialists. The advantage of including analyses of these multiple categories in a core course is that students have the opportunity to address central concerns of United States society within a shared framework of reading, analysis, and dialogue.

The syllabi chosen as illustrations in this guide indicate the degree to which the work of women writers and information about women's experiences in different cultures is being integrated into Western or world studies. There has been progress over the past two decades; women writers often are represented by at least one text per course. Gender also is used in many cases as a subtheme under larger thematic categories, such as in the courses at Brandeis University (see pages 24–25). However, much more historical and literary scholarship on women exists than is reflected in text selections in most of the core programs in the study; professional journals in virtually all disciplines include articles on this scholarship.

Women's history in particular came to the attention of the academy at large as early as the 1970s, when learned societies such as the Organization of American Historians and the American Historical Association began sponsoring projects and panels at annual meetings designed to incorporate gender into Western Civilization and world studies.[14] Many women's centers based at research universities have conducted projects aimed at integrating gender into general-education courses.[15] Women's studies remains a fruitful area of faculty development in the future.

Religion and religious values. In conjunction with their own missions, many independent institutions in the Cultural Legacies project sought to foster moral and religious values in students; faculty members selected ideas and texts in the humanities core to fulfill these aims. At the College of St. Francis, for example, Catholic and Franciscan contributions

SUNY–BUFFALO

AMERICAN PLURALISM AND THE SEARCH FOR EQUALITY

Goals for Students

1. The course should build on the understanding of world cultures developed in the World Civilization course.
2. A goal of the course is to develop within students a sense of informed, active citizenship as they enter an American society of increasing diversity by focusing on contemporary and historical issues of race, ethnicity, gender, social class, and religious sectarianism in American life.
3. A goal of the course is to provide students with an intellectual awareness of the causes and effects of structured inequalities and prejudicial exclusion in American society.
4. A goal of the course is to provide students with increased self-awareness of what it means in our culture to be a person of their own gender, race, class, ethnicity, and religion as well as an understanding of how these categories affect those who are different from themselves.
5. The issues introduced by the course need to be understood not in isolation but in the context of American institutions, history, culture, and values.
6. The five categories of race, ethnicity, gender, social class, and religion need to be understood not in isolation but as these categories overlap.
7. A goal of the course is to introduce students to the diversity of significant scholarship focusing on issues of race, gender, ethnicity, class, and religious differences.
8. A goal of the course is to expand students' ability to think critically, and with an open mind, about controversial contemporary issues that stem from gender, race, class, ethnic, and religious differences that pervade American society.
9. A curriculum on diversity must bring about an awareness of the enriching aspects of cultural pluralism as well as mutual respect for the integrity of other people's life experiences.
10. A goal of the course is to provide students with an intellectual awareness of diverse visions of the future as well as processes leading to a more equitable society.
11. The course should provide a common intellectual experience for undergraduate students.

to Western culture and thought receive special emphasis in the core curriculum. In addition to acquiring social awareness and ethical understanding, a "liberally educated student should understand the Judeo-Christian theological tradition and the importance of religion in human life," according to the core curriculum proposal. The Christian perspective is a central element in a three-semester sequence on the Western tradition.

Similarly at Samford University, the Christian perspective is an integrating thread throughout the core curriculum, which also features a strong curricular focus on developing personal values and behaviors. The freshman cultural legacies courses run in tandem with a year-long interdisciplinary course, "Personal Wholeness," which focuses on interpersonal, family, and community relationships; health; and the development of a responsible Christian life. A sophomore "Personal Wholeness" course focuses on Biblical perspectives and their significance for students' lives.

The junior core courses at Mount St. Mary's College focus on students' heritages and choices as citizens and residents of the United States and as people shaped by religious belief. In a year-long course called "The American Experience"—taught by English and history instructors—students explore how interactions of race, ethnicity, gender, and social class have modified European traditions. Two theology courses allow students to distinguish the insights and moral demands of Christianity, to read the Bible in a historical-critical and theological way, and to consider the Catholic intellectual tradition as a possible stance from which to make life choices.

On many campuses, introducing the religions of other cultures becomes a means to assist students to understand the role of religion in human lives and societies. It also is a popular way of exploring commonality across history and cultures. At Wesleyan College in Georgia, the new two-semester course, "The Emergence of the Modern World, 1500 to the Present," considers philosophy and religion as central to the study of Europe, Latin America, India, the Middle East, China, Africa, and Japan. The Integrative Studies Program at Otterbein College includes both lower-division and upper-division requirements in religion and philosophy—one focusing on Human Nature in the Christian Tradition and the other on Human Nature in Non-Western Religions or the Philosophy of Human Nature.

CONCEPTUAL PITFALLS: MISCONCEIVING THE "OTHER"

Faculty members teaching multiple cultural traditions within core studies discovered inherent problems in the (Western) construct "Western/non-Western." Many see this pairing as problematic because it can suggest monolithic and opposing cultural entities. As faculty members writing a critique of the core proposal at one institution note:

> [T]he proposal...defines the "second" or "other" culture as primarily and essentially "non-Western." In doing so, it treats "other" cultures as interchangeable blocks.... This procedure reinforces the notion that other cultures are interesting for contrast, not for their unique cultural content and not for the internal complexity and contradictions that characterized genuine cultural expression.

Another conceptual problem arises when faculty members introduce other cultures to show just how "West" the West is. The second culture becomes defined not as a presence in and of itself but as an absence or negation of what is Western. Faculty members at an institution that abandoned this approach wrote in their core world history course proposal:

> We have come to realize that we might unintentionally reinforce existing stereotypes by maintaining separate and inviolable "West" and "non-West" categories. Such a rigid distinction would allow students to continue to think in terms of "us" and "them," and "we" being "natural" and "they" being "exotic and strange." This would defeat one of the principal aims of curriculum reform—to foster in our students greater sensitivity to cultural pluralism.

This approach becomes more problematic when the cultural paradigms chosen to organize a course define other cultures only through their interaction with the West: for example, studying the "golden age" of a particular culture, then the moment the culture comes under stress from Western colonialism, and then the culture's response to Western influence or control. This response often is couched in terms of technological or social progress, while ignoring cultural continuities.

Another similarly problematic approach involves teaching heavily humanities-based Western culture courses—emphasizing art, philosophy, religion, and literature—and then teaching social science-oriented courses on "nondominant" or "minority" cultures. The message here is that Western culture is timeless, above societal pressures and idiosyncrasies, whereas other cultures arise from social and political pressures and are embedded in the immediacy of historical moments—hence not universal and timeless.

Viewing the contributions and experiences of different cultural groups from the perspective of the mainstream also may define the groups studied as powerless—focusing on the "plight" or "special problems" of these groups. Even if structures of domination are analyzed with the intent of illuminating the reasons for power and status differentials, the overall effect may be less than desirable. These approaches may lead to tensions among diverse students in the classroom due to the implicit hierarchies of value they convey. Students from the dominant culture may feel guilty, get defensive, and exhibit denial or anger, while students from "oppressed" groups may react negatively to analyses that cast them as solely "victims."

SUMMARY

Most of the institutions in the Cultural Legacies project avoided these pitfalls and overcame both stereotypes and simplistic dichotomies. They did so by employing a relational, not just a comparative, approach to the study of different cultures and of different perspectives within a society. Many of the new core courses explore multiple perspectives on the same set of events or dimensions of human experience, cultural dialogues and exchanges, or cultural encounters and conflicts. There is a discernible trend as well toward connecting the subject matter of cultural legacies courses with students' own immediate experiences, values, or assumptions. The new core courses attempt to make students aware of how their historical and cultural positions are connected to and different from those of people from other places and times.

This understanding of both difference and connection—of relationship—is at the heart of the transformation that the new core studies are effecting. In such approaches, different voices may occupy the center of attention for specific times; they are studied on their own terms, as viewed from within the culture. Traditions and cultures, Western and world, are viewed critically but not judgmentally. For other purposes and at other times, themes might be chosen to compare cultures and illuminate differing world views and perspectives, as well as influences, borrowings, intersections, or relationships among them. Johnnella Butler sees the identification of the connections between and interactions among disciplines and among cultures as a means of approximating, if not achieving, wholeness in the curriculum.[16]

For institutions just beginning to introduce diverse cultural traditions into core curricula, the variations found in the Cultural Legacies project may appear overwhelming. These institutions still are very much "in process" as they explore ways to address the multiple challenges of content selection. Their experiences, however, do illustrate three fundamental principles of good practice in including the study of diverse cultures in core curricula:

- clarity about goals for student learning
- distinctions among the objectives for the study of world cultures, Western society, and cultural pluralism in the United States
- models for a relational approach rather than an additive approach to the study of cultural experiences and human differences.

2 Core Structure and Pedagogy: More Challenges

▶ Teachers educate as much by how they teach as by what they teach.[17]

▶ New content on cultural pluralism engages faculty members and students as co-learners and encourages new classroom roles for both.

▶ The accomplishment of educational goals is related as much to the structure of programs as to content and pedagogy.

The real story in AAC's Cultural Legacies project is not that cultural pluralism is central to the new core curricula but that this new content is serving as a means for reconsidering the structure and pedagogy of undergraduate education. Core curriculum planners are experimenting in deliberate and systematic ways with interdisciplinary and thematic approaches, with new forms of student interaction and involvement in the learning process, and with connecting learning across courses and curricula. Recent research has shown that all of these practices correlate positively with students' intellectual development and maturation in college.[18]

The majority of the institutions in the Cultural Legacies project give pedagogical concerns equal standing with new content in the reform of core programs. Nearly all the new courses are interdisciplinary, based on primary texts, and thematically organized. Many make imaginative use of the arts. The core planning committees purposefully include faculty members well-versed in collaborative learning, interdisciplinary learning communities, and different teaching and learning styles—as the structures and pedagogy they have adopted indicate.

THE STRUCTURE OF CORE PROGRAMS

In her introduction to *Liberating Education*, Zelda Gamson suggests that "education with real power is based on structures as well as philosophies.

Structures constrain and direct what is taught and how."[19] In the Cultural
Legacies project, we found examples of three models for the structure of
core curricula: introductory core courses, vertically sequenced core programs, and course clusters. Issues of commonality and interdisciplinary
approaches arise in all these models.

Introductory core courses. The focus of the Cultural Legacies
project was introductory core courses—those that introduce students to
history, culture, civilization, and their meanings, as well as to the study of
significant texts. Such introductory courses serve as the foundation for student learning in general-education programs.

The University of Richmond's "Exploring Human Experience" is
an excellent example (see pages 20–21). It is a two-semester, interdisciplinary, six-credit, humanities course designed as an intensive introduction
to college-level study. Two hundred students—about one-third of the first-
year class—enrolled in the pilot course (1991–92); they were divided into
sections of fifteen students, each led by a faculty member. In the first year,
faculty members teaching the course came from twelve of the university's
eighteen arts and sciences departments. When fully implemented, the
course will integrate texts from the West, East Asia, Africa, and the Middle
East. All sections of "Exploring Human Experience" have a common syllabus, and all students read the same texts at the same times.

The course structure allows different kinds of learning experiences.
Students participate in individual tasks, such as writing in class; take part
in group learning in their section; meet periodically with two other section
groups; and frequently attend common cultural events that are part of the
course. They encounter differing perspectives on the material, given the
high degree of collaborative learning in most classes and the many disciplines the faculty members represent. Students report that they continue
their learning outside of class by comparing the perspectives they get from
different instructors.

The Richmond planning team worked hard to focus course goals
on what can be effectively accomplished in the credit hours available.
The course is designed as an "invitation" to college study. It introduces
students to significant texts from four major world cultures. Faculty members concentrate on teaching students to read texts, think critically, express
themselves clearly, and participate effectively in an intellectual community. Core planners have kept in mind that students have the rest of their
academic careers to expand their knowledge and skills and build on the
foundation laid in the core course.

Another good example is Oglethorpe University. There, "core" refers to a thirty-nine-credit grouping of courses linked by a common set of questions that invite students to examine "the material and spiritual challenges facing all of us today and formulate their own solutions to the human dilemma." A two-semester core history course serves as an introduction to the study of processes of political, economic, and cultural change. The course focuses on the interaction between Western and non-Western cultures and polities in two different periods of time: the medieval world and the modern world. Concentrating on these two periods introduces students to cultural comparisons. The course employs interactive methods in the classroom, using primary texts for analysis. Different sections of the course—averaging eighteen students each—are taught by full-time faculty members, who teach from an interdisciplinary perspective. Skills development is fostered by linking the course with a composition course.

Vertical core programs and capstone courses. In AAC's 1982 survey, *Reforming General Education*, Jerry Gaff and Thomas Klein reported that colleges and universities were making qualitative changes toward integration, global studies, a four-year course of study, and non-lecture pedagogy in general-education courses.[20] Institutions in the Cultural Legacies project demonstrate just how much progress is being made in extending core learning into upper division work. About half of the resource and planning institutions are designing core programs that sequence content and skills development into the junior or senior years.

Samford University's fifty-five-hour Cornerstone curriculum (see page 44) illustrates this trend. The twenty-hour Cultural Legacies component begins in the freshman year with the European Tradition, moving to The Non-Western World in the sophomore year and The American Experience in the junior year. Intermediate-level language and culture courses are placed in the freshman year to build on language study in high school. The study of science in the second year builds on concepts in mathematics. All core courses are tied into an interdisciplinary "personal wholeness" curriculum that spans all four years and emphasizes the interconnection of mind, body, and spirit. The rationale for this program is that professors can assume a base of student knowledge and competency and build upon it throughout the curriculum.

Washington State University's general-education program is organized vertically and horizontally in three tiers; elements of sequential study as well as distribution requirements are built into the curriculum. Tier I includes a two-semester sequence in "World Civilizations" that

SAMFORD UNIVERSITY
CORNERSTONE

20 hours: Breadth—Cultural Legacies
8 hours—I and II
The European Tradition: a two-semester course that views both Western and Eastern Europe from the Classical Age through the contemporary period, observed from the multiple perspectives of all humanities and fine arts disciplines, so that students may learn of the area's history and geography, its cultural manifestations (art, music, and literature), and its religious and political heritage. Bringing together a variety of teaching strategies and classroom activities, the courses move chronologically through time, reflecting the evolution of thought and tradition. Instruction in writing and speaking, provided in coordinated laboratory sessions, plays a prominent role in these freshman-level courses and builds a strong foundation for the remaining courses of the sequence.

6 hours—III and IV
The Non-Western World: two one-semester courses that take sophomores beyond the more familiar European scene into Africa and the East. Similar in format to Courses I and II, Course III, Africa and the Middle East, covers aspects of geography, history, religion, literature and the arts, and the sociopolitical organization of traditional African and Middle Eastern cultures across the centuries, while Course IV, Asia, explores similar aspects of the cultures of China, Japan, India, and Southeast Asia. As in Courses I and II, these courses are reading-, writing-, and speaking-intensive.

6 hours—V and VI
The American Experience: two one-semester courses that bring the study home to the western hemisphere and view the New World experience as a fusion of Old World traditions and native cultures. Both follow the same interdisciplinary perspective used in I–IV, but focus on the contributions of Europe, Africa, and the East to the multicultural heritage that is America's. Course V, Latin America, looks first at the pre-Columbian cultures, then moves through discovery, conquest, and colonizations to a comprehensive study of the distinctive Latin American nations of today. Course VI, The U.S.A., the capstone course of the sequence, traces major developments in North American society and thought, from its native cultures through the waves of immigration, and on to the contemporary scene. It places special emphasis on the increasingly pluralistic nature of our society and views the cultural diversity within the United States as a microcosm of all the world's peoples. Students continue to develop reading, writing, and speaking skills through the sequence's ongoing emphasis on these competencies.

8 hours: Depth—Foreign Language and Culture
Intermediate I and II
Language and Culture: a two-semester intermediate level course designed to develop crosscultural understanding and proficiency in speaking, understanding, reading, and writing within the target language's geographical and cultural context. These interactive class and lab sessions offer exposure to career-specific language designed for professionals in teaching, literature and the arts, intercultural communication, health care, business, social services, and ministry and mission. Students are encouraged to spend part of their Language and Culture Sequence at one of our study centers abroad.

provides the base for the program by giving students a common core of knowledge, introducing them to issues and methods in the humanities, and promoting a global perspective. Also in Tier I are English composition (linked to "World Civilizations"), mathematics, and introduction to science. Tier II consists of fifteen hours of distribution requirements in the sciences, social sciences, and humanities. For this tier, students must take courses within one of eight designated areas of coherence that serve to link courses within a conceptual framework. These areas are Foundations of Western Civilization; Foundations of the Modern World; American Cultures; Structures of Society; Human Values and Religions; Global Perspectives; Ecology and the Planet; and Science, Society, and Evolution. Courses in Tier III provide the final components of sequential study in general education by assisting students in integrating and synthesizing material from courses in both the major and general education and from nonacademic experiences.

With the emphasis on vertical sequencing and the desire to connect general education with learning in the major, more and more institutions are introducing capstone general-education courses as part of core learning. The Integrative Studies capstone course at Otterbein College engages three cultures. One of these is the mainstream culture of the majority of Otterbein students, contemporary United States culture; the second represents a historical aspect of cross-cultural encounter—the Spanish/indigenous peoples on this continent; and the third, an "other" culture: contemporary Japan. Through these cultures, the capstone course explores the relationship between language and culture; examines competencies and motives for knowing and empathizing with other cultures; includes an exploration of a current issue in American society related to cross-cultural encounters, such as bilingualism; and asks students to formulate an action plan for resolving the issue.

Queens College (N.C.) is developing, with a new NEH grant, a senior capstone course—the last course of its seven-course integrated vertical core—that will emphasize critical thinking and ethical theory. The course will utilize case studies selected to represent different areas of adult work: education, business, health care, and human services. Students will learn how to analyze problems and develop solutions to complex societal issues. George Mason University has proposed a senior seminar dealing with moral and sociopolitical issues; faculty members at the College of St. Francis have approved a capstone to connect learning in the liberal arts core with work in the major.

Faculty planners are optimistic that these programs will allow them to develop among students a base of knowledge and skills that they can build upon in culminating senior year courses. Faculty members will be able to reach across courses to draw upon, enlarge, and connect learning for and with their students.

Course clusters. Developing a selection of course clusters to fulfill core requirements is a good solution for large institutions with great diversity and in which faculty members do not wish to adopt a single model for the core. The core program at Utah State University—the Liberal Arts and Sciences Program (LASP)—consists of sets of courses organized around a common interdisciplinary theme (to date, beauty, civilization, science and society, future environments). The program features lower- and upper-division requirements as well as electives and crosses the liberal arts and sciences. Each cluster culminates in a capstone course. Students must take a program orientation course and two LASP clusters to fulfill general-education requirements. To provide program coherence, an interdisciplinary faculty committee designs and oversees each cluster, and all faculty members participate in annual faculty development workshops.

The Cultural Legacies project team at Utah State is creating a Legacies cluster composed of existing and new courses. Its five tiers are Approaches to Legacies; Natural Legacies; Utah and the American West; Legacies of the United States; and World Legacies: Heterogeneity and Interdependency. The proposed capstone, "Creating Legacies for the Twenty-First Century," includes a portfolio workshop in which students will review their work in the Legacies cluster and prepare a final paper on their learning experiences. This new Legacies cluster combines sciences and the liberal arts to explore themes of diversity and tradition.

Clustered courses also are an option at the University of California–Los Angeles. The humanities course clusters being developed through AAC's Cultural Legacies project consist of three general-education courses that are thematically, historically, or theoretically related. In the fall of 1991, a freshman cluster and an upper-division cluster were piloted. In the freshman cluster, "The Art and Literature of Western Antiquity," students enrolled in normally scheduled general-education courses: Art History 50A, Ancient Art; Humanities 1A, World Literature from Antiquity to the Early Middle Ages; and English 3, Rhetoric and Language. To ensure integration, students enrolled in the cluster were assigned to a special section of English 3; this writing seminar was redesigned to focus on the materials in the other courses in the cluster. Students also enrolled in a special discussion section attached to the history course. All faculty members in the cluster attended occasional section meetings to give differing perspectives on the cluster material. Cooperative learning experiences are introduced through projects that students complete outside of class.

The upper-division cluster, "Manipulations of Sign Systems," included Philosophy 31, Logic; Linguistics 100, Introduction to Linguistics; and English 129, Intermediate Exposition. Additional clusters piloted in 1992 include Latin American Literature and History, Native American Culture, and Encountering the Other: Spain and America. The UCLA experiments with humanities clusters have been facilitated by the existence of the Writing Program, which has a long history of developing collaborative learning projects, linked courses, and learning communities.

These cluster models are intellectually rich while allowing students flexibility of choice. They provide a common core for a group of students who experience the benefits of cooperative and collaborative learning.[21]

Commonality covenants. Traditions of faculty autonomy work against commonality in core programs. Even in courses with the same name, faculty members in different sections often teach quite different syllabi. Developing programs of common study requires, quite literally, new social contracts among faculty members.

Curriculum planners in the Cultural Legacies project made very different decisions on the desirability of a high degree of commonality depending on their institutional culture, resources, and the amount of value placed on faculty autonomy. University Studies in the Humanities at Brandeis University is a good example of limited commonality. The program offers a selection of courses in two steps: Step I courses cover Ancient and Classical Civilizations; Step II courses cover Modern Topics. Step I courses must include one Homeric text, one text from the Hebrew Bible, and one New Testament text; Step II courses must include work by two authors from this list: Dante, Shakespeare, Diderot, Austen, Dickinson, Freud, and Fanon.

Washington State University (WSU) has pursued a more extensive base of common study. To ensure commonality across sections in its World Civilizations course, WSU faculty members have developed for themselves a "Covenant of Coverage and Course Objectives" (see pages 48–49). This document specifies that all World Civilizations course sections—each one entirely taught by one professor—be global and comparative, be divided at the year 1500, be interdisciplinary in content and methodology, be linked through common readings, and include certain common assignments, such as a library research assignment. The covenant also specifies which civilizations and subtopics must be included in each section. The covenant represents an interesting effort, unusual for a large university, to make the

WASHINGTON STATE UNIVERSITY

THE COVENANT (of Coverage and Course Objectives
for World Civilizations 110–111)

Course Objectives
1. To provide coherent intellectual frameworks for subsequent learning.
2. To provide students a common body of basic knowledge concerning the origins and development of human cultures, with an emphasis on the major world civilizations.
3. To enhance students' awareness, understanding, and appreciation of the great art, thoughts, and achievements of human beings living under an enormous variety of conditions.
4. To encourage students to develop a broad international perspective on historical and cultural developments as a background for understanding the contemporary world.
5. To develop students' abilities to recognize and to analyze problems; to think critically and to ask questions; to synthesize diverse kinds of information and to express their ideas clearly and cogently.
6. To teach students basic library research skills and information retrieval.
7. To introduce students to some of the basic methodologies in the scholarly disciplines.
8. To encourage students to attend cultural events.

Course Guidelines
All sections of World Civilizations 110–111 must:
1. Be global and comparative in approach.
2. Be divided at 1500 and—in each course—treat the civilizations and subtopics appropriate to each, as specified below.
3. Be interdisciplinary in content, giving attention in each major civilization to its material base (geography, economy, subsistence system); its social system (kinship, gender, class, politics); its ideological system (religion, science, philosophy); creative arts (literature, music, visual arts, architecture); and its continuity and stability/change over time.
4. Be interdisciplinary in methodology, drawing upon the structures of the several disciplines in the humanities and social sciences to introduce frames of reference; to analyze questions/problems; to identify theories, generalizations, concepts; to synthesize, interpret facts.
5. Be linked through common readings (e.g., textbooks, collections of readings).
6. Have a graded library assignment and exams that contain an essay component. Gen Ed 111 must have a cultural events assignment.

(All instructors in World Civilizations 110 and 111 are required to include the following civilizations and subtopics as minimum requirements.)

World Civilizations 110

Civilizations	Subtopics
Earliest Civilizations	1. Mesopotamia
	2. Egypt
	3. Indus
	4. Yellow River
South Asia (India)	1. Hinduism/Buddhism
	2. Muslim incursion
East Asia (China and Japan)	1. Confucianism and Taoism
	2. Buddhism
	3. Heian Japan
Europe	1. Homeric Age
	2. Classical Greece
	3. Hellenistic Greece
	4. Rome: Republic and Empire
	5. Medieval Europe
	6. Italian Renaissance
Middle East and Africa	1. Development of Judaism
	2. Development of Christianity
	3. Rise of Islam
	4. Spread of Islam
Americas	Pre-Columbian Cultures

Note: The course should begin with a unit on the background and origins of civilization, with attention to geography and world cultures before civilizations arose.

World Civilizations 111

Civilizations	Subtopics
South Asia (India)	1. Mughal
	2. British
	3. Independence
East Asia (China and Japan)	1. Manchu China
	2. Tokugawa Japan
	*3. Opening to the West
	4. Nationalism and Socialism
Europe	1. Northern Renaissance and Reformation
	2. Scientific Revolution and Enlightenment
	*3. Maritime Expansion and Exploration
	4. Absolutism and Revolution
	5. Romanticism and Nationalism
	6. Industrialism and Socialism
	*7. World Wars I & II
Middle East and North Africa	1. Ottoman Empire
	2. Imperialism and Nationalism
Sub-Saharan Africa	1. Pre-Colonial and Slave Trade
	2. Colonialism
	3. Nationalism
Americas	1. Discovery and Settlement
	2. Appropriate ties to related European topics (e.g., revolution, nationalism)

*These topics have global and international dimensions.

Note: The course should end with several class sessions devoted to contemporary issues (e.g., environment, science and values, mass culture, arms race).

World Civilizations course a genuinely common program while still allowing faculty members substantial autonomy in the ways they weave the common subject matter together to compose the syllabi for their individual sections.

Fairleigh Dickinson University and Queens College (N.C.) represent the most encompassing approach to commonality—including a common topical syllabus, common readings, examinations and assignments in sections of the core courses. All faculty members teaching in the core meet biweekly to coordinate presentations and assignments; they also prepare exams together. At Queens, because faculty members emphasize different perspectives in their sections, a percentage of each examination is section-specific.

Richard Guarasci, dean of Hobart College at Hobart and William Smith Colleges and former director of the First-Year Program at St. Lawrence University, outlines some of the advantages of commonality:

> Our commitment to a thematically based common course brings us together as a faculty struggling to uncover our respective voices *within* the program as well as our common voice *as* a program. To separate ourselves into twelve separate courses would end the intellectual community that we, the faculty, are becoming within the program. While commonality can become a straitjacket that crushes creativity and spontaneity, we must continue to risk that our collective common sense will prevent the strangulation of intellectual growth among the program faculty. Without a common course, teams will be drawn from those sharing similar interests as well as temperaments, with the probable long run results of re-fragmenting all of us back into our parochial identities. We can easily undo the inclusive conversations we now must undertake, as "interest and creativity" overtake the messiness of developing sensitivity, and ultimately, interest in previously unknown subjects.[22]

After a five-year experiment with common readings in all course sections, St. Lawrence recently has decided to adopt tight guidelines but no required, shared readings. Through a five-day planning session for all those who teach the course, however, faculty members emerge with a shared understanding of what the course is trying to accomplish, the kinds of books that will serve their goals, and how best to teach them. Thus, there is, in Guarasci's words, "a socially-constructed commonality, not an imposed, required commonality."

A significant degree of commonality has serious implications for faculty workload. Faculty members who teach in these programs have to commit themselves to collaborative work with their colleagues, especially if there are common assignments and examinations. For example, at the University of North Carolina–Asheville, all faculty members in the core program attend the weekly lecture, given by one of them, and then discuss central material to highlight in all individual sections. Resources are necessary to compensate faculty members appropriately for this level of involvement.

The histories of the resource institutions in the Cultural Legacies project suggest, however, that it is possible—although difficult—to sustain a high degree of commonality even in a long-established core program. Four of the eleven resource institutions in the Cultural Legacies project— Columbia University, University of Kansas, University of North Carolina– Asheville, and Earlham College—have sustained core curricula for more than twenty-five years. While these programs have evolved substantially over time, all have been able to sustain a high degree of community and commonality among faculty members teaching in their core courses. The secret, as we shall explore in Chapters 3 and 4, is a combination of strong leadership, institutional commitment, and a variety of strategies that keep faculty members learning with and from one another.

Interdisciplinary approaches. AAC's Cultural Legacies project provided support for the development of core curricula in the humanities. Consequently, institutions selected to participate had strong humanities-based programs. The interesting trend in these programs, however, is that nearly all institutions are attempting to use interdisciplinary study to elucidate the complexity and richness of a culture, problem, or period of time. They claim interdisciplinary study as a pathway to connectedness for learners.

Interdisciplinary practice, as it is represented in the project, brings faculty members from different disciplinary and interdisciplinary bases together in a common effort to create new approaches to textual analysis. Core programs draw faculty members from many departments on campus. Whether the administrative structure has a core faculty—as in the case of the Undergraduate College at SUNY–Buffalo, in which fifty senior faculty members design and serve as advocates for the program—or informally draws faculty members together weekly to discuss course materials, there is a beneficial interplay between each faculty member's disciplinary knowledge and the interdisciplinary perspectives they gain from participation in core teaching. Historical information, textual analysis, sociological, philosophical, and political perspectives all are brought to bear on the elucidation of texts and cultures under study. Students see models of how faculty members trained in different disciplines bring their own perspectives to the understanding of the topics presented in the course. Faculty members can draw better connections for their majors, knowing the kinds of experiences they have in the core programs.

Queens College (N.C.) provides a good illustration. In the first-year course of the Liberal Learning Program, which covers central texts and artifacts from antiquity to the Enlightenment, methods and approaches used are common to the humanities. In the sophomore course, which spans Western culture from the Enlightenment to the present, the teaching team includes faculty members from the social sciences. The course becomes more interdisciplinary as the perspectives from these disciplines are used to understand complex societies of the nineteenth and twentieth centuries.

For example, in the second term of the sophomore year there is a two-day unit on the civil rights movement in North Carolina. Readings include a reflective piece by James Baldwin, a journalistic account of the lunch counter sit-ins, an exploration of the relationship between the African American church and the civil rights movement, and "A Message to the Grass Roots" by Malcolm X. The course thus uses perspectives from literature, journalism, religion, and politics to elucidate an important event in United States and Southern history.

Interdisciplinary approaches also accomplish an important function related to creating intellectual community among faculty and students. The kinds of questions that are raised in course discussions require many different perspectives to address. Working in interdisciplinary communities, as Patrick Hill has pointed out, requires that we develop a new kind of collegiality, one characterized by "conversations of respect." In conversations of respect, he notes, participants sense a need for one another. These conversations are characterized by intellectual reciprocity: the individuals expect to learn from one another, to change intellectually, as a result of their encounter. One participant does not treat the other as an illustration or a variation upon a truth or insight already fully possessed by oneself. There is no will to incorporate others in any sense into one's personal belief system. Conversations of respect across significant differences, whether these differences are disciplinary or cultural, enhance one's awareness of being unable to answer a question on one's own. These are the kinds of questions that Hill believes are fundamental to the educational process.[23]

At some institutions, core planners are attempting to go beyond the disciplines. The core planners at Fairleigh Dickinson University call this approach "transdisciplinary." It challenges the ownership of texts by specific disciplines and attempts to forge a language and pedagogy that transcends any specific field.

CULTURAL PLURALISM AND SKILLS DEVELOPMENT

Well-integrated core curricula include careful attention by the faculty to the development and practice of skills they believe are essential for students to acquire during their undergraduate experience. AAC's *A New Vitality in General Education* calls for more precision in the definition of these skills, from a vague set of terms such as *understand* and *appreciate*— which imply that a student looks in at the world from the outside—to terms such as *describe, analyze, compare, critique, extend theory*, which imply student engagement with problems, issues, and questions from within the domains they encounter.[24] Three areas of skills development are particularly salient in the Cultural Legacies project.

Writing. The new core courses are, for the most part, writing-intensive. Here we see clearly the extensive impact of writing-across-the-curriculum programs over the past two decades. There is hardly an institution in the project that has not had such a program. Many are strongly committed to writing development and have created and staffed writing laboratories. Faculty development programs often include sessions on writing techniques for faculty members who have yet not learned to incorporate writing as a learning process in the classroom.

Some core programs require students to take necessary skills courses in writing, communication, and mathematics before beginning the core program. This is the case at LeMoyne-Owen College, where students show competencies through placement tests or complete Core I Studies in critical thinking, reading, writing, speech, and mathematics (which carry no credit for graduation) before beginning Core II, of which the Human Heritage sequence is a part. Similarly, at SUNY–Buffalo, students must pass or exempt-out of foundational writing and library skills in their freshman year. Another solution is to integrate writing into all of the courses in the core program. The Earlham College Humanities Program offers a good example of writing-intensive core courses. Groups of five to six students gather for weekly writing workshops in which they analyze and discuss each other's papers.

Other institutions in the Cultural Legacies project are experimenting with linking core humanities courses to a writing course. Almost invariably, core curriculum planners want students to learn to read critically and to write analytic papers based on primary sources. This means, however, that class assignments may begin to duplicate some of the work being done in English composition courses. Linking the Cultural Legacies course or courses with a writing course substantially extends the number of opportunities students have to build competence in reading and writing about difficult texts and topics.

The goals of studying cultural pluralism are facilitated by working with English faculty members, many of whom have, over the years, been involved with initiatives to incorporate race, class, gender, and ethnicity as a means of connecting students' personal and academic work through writing. The Freshman Seminar at Lesley College, "Leadership and Ethics in the Professions," introduces students to the basic methodologies of historical research, literary criticism, and philosophical and ethical inquiry through assignments such as the "cultural autobiography," in which students explore and write about their own particular cultural legacies referencing general research and family interviews.

In a pilot version of a core curriculum at George Mason University, students begin in the first semester with paired courses: Core 100, Composition for Communication, and Core 103, the Presence of the Past (a first course in Western culture). The strategy here is to strengthen the writing course by having students develop oral communications skills through small-group work and by linking these skills with specific content from texts read in Core 103. This paired approach creates small student learning communities that work on projects outside of class.

Coordination at Washington State University appears to offer a good pedagogical solution to concerns in both "World Civilizations" and "English Composition." Resource constraints made it impossible to teach "World Civilizations" in small sections; English 101 is universally required of all freshmen and taught in small discussion-group format but lacked a defining theme. Faculty planners saw clear advantages to coordinating the two courses. Not only would this coordination make better use of students' precious reading and thinking time but skills and content knowledge could be reinforced and strengthened by foregrounding them in one course and backgrounding them in the other.

To achieve this goal, a faculty member in the English Department organized a graduate seminar on curriculum development in which students helped select materials for the course and prepared to teach it. The selection of readings has subsequently been published under the title *Writing about the World.*[25] These readings are complementary to, but not part of, Washington State's "World Civilizations" courses, although students are encouraged to make connections. One of the central assignments in the writing course is a library paper on intercultural issues which builds upon the question-analysis library search technique taught in "World Civilizations." Another assignment is a paper critiquing one of the campus cultural events required for students in the Civilizations course.

Critical thinking. Nearly every institution in the Cultural Legacies project included the development of students' critical thinking skills as a central goal of the core curriculum. The focus on cultural diversity and difference proved to be an excellent means of eliciting critical reflections—what Elizabeth Minnich speaks of as "welcoming the disruptions of diversity":

> With discussion, they awaken reflection, reflexivity, critical thinking, imagination, and judgment; they call on us to exercise these human/humane virtues not only in the study of texts but also on institutions and systems, on habits of practice, as of the heart, as of the mind. Diversity as confrontation with the very differences most invidiously constructed among us is invaluable in startling us into thought at the deepest levels, the levels on which we remember why education matters in and for the world beyond our professions.[26]

Direct engagement with the realities of cultural difference, as manifested in both individual and group habits and commitments, can foster the development of skills of analysis, interpretation, and judgment. Engagement with cultural difference means challenging the root assumptions, paradigms, values, and world views upon which cultures are built and calling into questions the construction of meaning within cultures themselves. These confrontations with deep-seated assumptions challenge us to go well beyond what we normally call into question when we speak of the Western tradition as self-critical.

Core directors and faculty members at institutions with core curricula that extend over two or more years have begun to sequence skill development across the core. They are accomplishing this task by articulating specific exercises in skill development from course to course, building on students' knowledge, skills, and competencies as they progress through the core curriculum.

The sixty-one-hour core curriculum—roughly half the curriculum—at Mount St. Mary's College (Md.) is tightly sequenced across these interrelated dimensions. Students study the Western tradition in history, literature, the arts, and philosophy during their freshman and sophomore years; they examine United States culture in the junior year and non-Western culture in the senior year. Students reflect on values questions and their own values systems in the year-long Freshman Seminar before embarking on full-year explorations of philosophy (sophomore year), theology (junior year), and ethical theory (senior year). Methodologically, students concentrate on critical thinking skills in Freshman Seminar and discipline-based freshman- and sophomore-year courses before proceeding to the interdisciplinary junior- and senior-year courses. Writing, speaking, and research skills are emphasized throughout the curriculum.

The core program at Earlham College is an example of especially well-developed and intentional sequencing of skills. Earlham provides each first-year student with a sixty-six-page booklet that spells out in detail the program's expectations for students' intellectual development. The booklet describes the rationale for the four-course Humanities Program and how teaching and learning activities vary from term to term.

In Humanities I sections, limited to twenty-three students, students read one text per week and write a paper about it before the first class discussion of the book. The objectives of both the paper and the class discussions are to teach students to identify the major ideas in the text, to determine the author's position on these ideas and reasons for holding those positions, and to develop their own positions on the issues and rationales for these positions. The Humanities Program booklet includes a chapter on the Humanities I paper and appendices on the mechanics of paper writing and on argument and inquiry.

Humanities II–III is a two-term sequence in which historical and literary works are studied separately and comparatively, in chronological order. These courses are designed to build on the dialogic skills learned in Humanities I by teaching students to comprehend texts through intensive analysis—to explain the whole by examining the parts and how they are interrelated.

Humanities IV students, having attained a well-integrated background in the historical dimensions of culture, delve deeper into either history and literature *as a discipline,* by selecting one course from an approved list. This intensive study within the boundaries of a particular discipline is designed to help students distinguish between the unique methods of that discipline and the general humanistic background out of which it emerged.

Numerous other institutions in the Cultural Legacies project view the sequences in their core programs developmentally. Queens College

(N.C.), the University of North Carolina–Asheville, and several others with senior courses view the capstone courses as opportunities for students to further develop and apply analytic, ethical, and problem-solving capabilities to complex human and social questions. It is extremely rare, however, to find faculty members spelling out the requirements for critical thinking and other skill-related course assignments in the kind·of detail established by Earlham's Humanities Program. There remains a need for the same kind of covenants regarding course practices and assignments that Washington State has established in relation to common course content.

Civic competencies. Nationally, there has been little explicit attention in general education to preparing students to be members of collectivities. Faculties seem guided by a deep-seated assumption that the liberal arts education in and of itself—through teaching students about complex historic and contemporary issues facing societies; developing their intellectual capacities to reason and make judgements, argue soundly, and express themselves clearly; and exposing them to values such as liberty, justice, equality, the common good—creates educated and good citizens.

Cultural diversity has immensely complicated issues of civic literacy and competencies. Michael Morris identifies central issues:

> [H]ow will we work to insure that the different voices get heard and expressed in the democratic system? How do we create the mechanisms, the forums for new multicultural conversations?...
>
> [W]hat learning experience ought a student have if s/he is a member of the current dominant group in our society, or if s/he is a member of a culturally diverse group? Regardless of race, how important is it going to be for folks to truly encounter people different from themselves? How important will it be to go beyond one's self, one's own identity, one's previous cultural and class experience?[27]

Morris lists necessary new civic competencies: interdependence; collaboration; holistic vision; cross-cultural communications; multicultural awareness; consensus-decision making; community-global thinking; bilingualism and multilingualism; ecological perspective; and racism, sexism, and oppression awareness.

A few of the institutions in the Cultural Legacies project are incorporating the development of civic competencies into their core curricula. A large section of the Queens College (N.C.) first-year core course is devoted to issues of human community; students read and discuss texts on human rights and responsibilities, law, civil disobedience, ideal order and temporal justice. The sophomore-level course treats issues in the modern world, with special emphasis on United States society from the Salem witch trials through the gay rights movement.

The core at the University of Alaska–Fairbanks includes a course area, "Values and Choice," that seeks to develop in students an understanding of how individuals come to hold the values they proclaim. It introduces students to differences in values systems within various world cultures and focuses on helping students understand the dilemmas of moral choice affecting individuals in complex societies.

St. Lawrence University's First-Year Program, conducted in residential colleges, emphasizes the interconnection of community and personal development. Three faculty members from three different departments teach the first-year course, "The Human Condition: Nature, Self and Society." Each faculty member has ten to fifteen students in seminars twice per week. In addition, all students and faculty members meet as a group twice a week. The program emphasizes the role of education in the formation of character:

> We work to create a community as we respect privacy and individuality and as we recognize common experience as the basis of public domain. Liberal education should mean something that is a new version of an older ideal: the forging of a democratic community where individuals learn to create both an authentic self and a series of socially responsible publics that extend from the local milieux to the global village.[28]

The reading list for "The Human Condition" intentionally draws together classics from the Western tradition with feminist critiques of that tradition and with perspectives on human community drawn from other cultures and societies. The residential environment becomes at once a living and a learning community forged out of diversity.

Historically black institutions, with their special mission of creating supportive environments for students who have faced barriers to full participation in society, have long-standing traditions of instilling civic competencies, using core humanities study to encourage the development in students of behaviors associated with leadership and good citizenship. Spelman College, for example, is intentional in developing leadership and service qualities in its students. Spelman's goals for student learning include demonstrating an understanding of and sensitivity to the multicultural communities of the world, a sense of responsibility for bringing about positive change in those communities, and a willingness to serve the community. These goals could well serve to guide predominantly white institutions in developing civic expectations and competencies of students who—if they are to lead in a multicultural world—also need training in the competencies that Morris suggests.

NEW PEDAGOGIES

"We are reaching a new consensus that the primary aim of Heritage Studies is the empowerment of our students, rather than the transmission of a body of cultural/historical information," writes David Krause, director of Heritage Studies at Carthage College, in a final report on Carthage's participation in the Cultural Legacies project. The pedagogies used in core programs are becoming increasingly learner-centered as faculty members develop different teaching approaches that emphasize active student involvement and collaborative learning. Collaborative learning emphasizes social and intellectual engagement and responsibility in an attempt to counteract many current ills of the curriculum: the distance between faculty members and students, over-reliance on the lecture method, student passivity, and students' alienation from each other and from their learning processes.[29]

In the programs that have adopted collaborative approaches, faculty members act more like facilitators than experts. Their role is to guide students in their exploration of texts, not predetermine what is of interest and importance. This method allows students to see their own and the teacher's learning processes. A faculty member might handle a question this way: "I don't know the answer to that question, but this might be a part of it. I'll check and see what I can find." In setting these expectations for teaching style, program leaders assume that faculty members are teachers not solely of subject matter but of learning modes and habits of mind.

Faculty members in these programs are what they hope students become: life-long learners. For example, Jennifer Nourse, anthropologist, University of Richmond, writes of her encounter with Nietzsche's *On the Genealogy of Morals*:

> In addition to forcing me to learn to read again, the text allowed me to empathize with my students. I recalled what it was like to be a freshman grappling with difficult material. Like them, I feared humiliation: Could I make sense of this and not make a fool of myself in class? Luckily, I did not have to prove myself an authority since the core course was designed to avoid the authoritative voice. This relaxed environment led me to be honest with my students: "I had

difficulty reading this, but found a way to make sense of it. What reading process did you use?" I conveyed my learning process and they conveyed theirs. Not only did we study Nietzsche's message, but we learned a skill together.[30]

Core program directors have often found that ethnic studies and women's studies faculty members are indispensable sources of energy and enthusiasm for these pedagogical approaches because of their history of student-centered teaching and learning. The early stages of feminist and black studies pedagogy sought to build on experiences familiar to their specific student populations. Influenced by Paolo Friere and others, faculty members developed teaching practices that valued the individual student's experience as a base of knowledge to complement textual materials, challenged hierarchical modes of teaching, and taught students to take responsibility for their own learning. They discovered that difference can be a fruitful means of collaboration among students who must negotiate with one another across significant differences to perform a task or resolve a problem.

Models for collaborative learning gained considerable ground in the early 1980s. Romer described the benefits of the new paradigm for teaching and learning:

> Collaborative models bring to education a kind of parity between student and faculty: they see themselves as contributing differing perspectives, being allied exactly because they will not see things from the same vantage point. If the collaborative process merely transforms the student into mini-teacher, clone, of disciple of the authority, the goals of collaborative learning have not been achieved by student or teacher. Each must recognize that the perspectives and experience of the other will contribute to the process of teaching and learning by which knowledge is affirmed, refashioned, or made anew.[31]

Gamson and Hill have articulated some of the benefits of new faculty roles in their analysis of how to create a lively academic community. These new roles minimize faculty members' psychological distance from students and make faculty members more accessible to students. At the same time, curricular structures "legitimize both the accessibility and the authority of the teachers." When programs are built upon discourse and critical thinking, students can both engage and disagree with faculty members in the daily life of programs.[32]

The introduction of new core curricula exploring diverse cultures has provided an optimal situation for collaborative learning, since faculty members in these programs are themselves students of new subject matter.

At the University of Richmond, for example, faculty members employ collaborative learning activities—such as small-group work in which students generate central questions about the readings—almost exclusively. They make no secret of the fact that they are co-learners with the students and that they are working together to explore questions the texts raise. One Richmond student speculates that not all faculty members would be suited to teach in the new core course, because "we—the students—are in charge; it's our ideas that matter." In interviews, faculty members praise the new methods as more intellectually stimulating and rewarding for students, who practice skills in summary, critique, analysis, and theory-building—all of which are viewed as fundamental to the continuation of their learning in their undergraduate years and beyond.

This emphasis on discussion and group work does not mean that the lecture mode is not also an effective means of teaching—just that it has its limitations and must be balanced with opportunities for other kinds of learning experiences. Lecturing still is used extensively in these core programs. Nor does collaborative learning mean that faculty members abandon their leadership role in the classroom; "student-centered" is not the same as "student-directed." It takes a very skilled faculty member to guide students to learn through collaborative learning activities.

These experiments with new faculty-student relationships in the learning process indicate that a shift in attitudes about student learning in the classroom is becoming noticeable on many campuses. There is less condescension toward students. Faculty members are changing their ideas about content acquisition and are seeing the inefficacy of blaming students for what they do not know and do not value. Faculty members see their role more as helping students connect course content with what students do know and care about, including themselves.[33]

The role of faculty member as "facilitator" or "co-learner" rather than "expert" resonates with the new focus on the individual as interdependent with the community in the Cultural Legacies project. Faculty members model effective relationships within a community (the classroom) characterized by those who are diversely situated relative to status and power. Students also learn to listen to their peers and gain insight into different perspectives on topics under discussion. With collaborative learning activities and their redefinition of the relation between individual and group effort, the Western paradigm of the individual learner comes into question. This shift toward valuing one's connection to and responsibility to others and toward cooperative modes of interaction challenges older U.S. societal norms of aggressive individualism and competitiveness.

CAVEATS

These new structures and pedagogies are not without drawbacks. Many of the programs in the Cultural Legacies project are experiencing negative reactions from both faculty members and students who are uncomfortable with changing roles in the classroom. Some students resist "empowerment"; interactive learning techniques that require active engagement with course materials and with faculty members and other students may make them feel provoked, exposed, or even used. Other students have an almost unshakable belief in the professor as the sole authority in the classroom and become frustrated when students talk too much. In developing learning goals and techniques, it is important for core courses to include many different types of activities to accommodate students' different learning styles. It also is important to take into account the developmental processes of students and adapt collaborative learning activities to students' stages of development.

Moreover, many faculty members prefer to retain more authority over content and its dissemination in the classroom. Those core programs that envisage active student involvement and collaborative learning as mainstays of course methods must clearly communicate these expectations to faculty members who teach in the program. They must invest in faculty development programs to assist faculty members in developing the necessary teaching skills.

TIPS FOR GOOD PRACTICE

As we have seen, there is a growing ethos of connection, collaboration, and community among faculty members and students associated with new core programs that engage cultural legacies and new pedagogies. A central benefit to designing programs that include opportunities for faculty interaction—such as joint teaching sessions, sitting in on one another's classes, or collaborative planning of syllabi and class sessions—is that faculty members share responsibility for student learning and see the possibilities for connections across courses. The new core courses, in short, illustrate a broadly based determination to challenge the intellectual fragmentation that has come to characterize undergraduate education.

Core planners who wish to create a structurally and pedagogically sound program must:

- recognize that content and pedagogy are inseparable and that learning goals for each need to be clearly articulated

- analyze the current structure of the core and/or general-education program and how well this structure fits program goals

- evaluate various options for program structure and choose one that fits program goals

- refrain from overburdening introductory courses with more learning goals that can be effectively accomplished in the available credit hours

- develop effective means of connecting learning across courses in the program, such as linked courses, interactive faculty planning, and learning communities

- use collaborative learning activities to develop intellectual and social community and responsibility among students

- invest in faculty development programs to assist faculty members in learning new collaborative learning techniques.

3 Faculty Development

▶ Imagine you are a new Ph.D. in Japanese history who has just become an assistant professor at Old Ivy, a prestigious liberal arts college. You have experience teaching basic courses in your field, but you are anxious about the expectations of your new department for both teaching and research. During your first week on campus you get a telephone call from the dean of the college who asks you to consider teaching in the new core humanities curriculum. All you have to do is read ten new texts, work with a team of faculty members from other departments, and teach an interdisciplinary, cross-cultural syllabus, the subject matter of which is almost entirely outside of your area. How could you decline such an opportunity?

The most striking characteristic of the new core programs incorporating diverse cultures is their redefinition of the uses of faculty expertise in the classroom. The courses in these programs ask faculty participants to venture outside their own specialties and acquire knowledge of new cultures and texts; competence in comparative studies; skill in interdisciplinary practices; and, for most campuses in the Cultural Legacies project, skills in the techniques of encouraging active student learning. To prepare faculty members to meet such ambitious expectations, campuses must commit themselves to strong faculty development programs and develop reward structures that appropriately recognize the contributions faculty members make to core programs.

Curricular change, ultimately, is faculty development. There can be no substantive change in the curriculum—be it introducing writing across the curriculum, "internationalizing" the curriculum, introducing the study of new cultures, indeed any major initiative—without faculty members engaging in an intellectual adventure that generates the necessary commitment and energy for making change. Institutions that attempt to revamp curricula without preparing faculty members to teach in the new programs are courting disaster.

Within the Cultural Legacies project, the most successful programs established systematic, long-term faculty development programs that were designed specifically around the different phases of curriculum development—planning, piloting, implementing, and sustaining the core program. These faculty development programs took into account differing faculty expertise, interests, and needs, and they provided appropriate incentives, resources, and rewards.

MOTIVATING FACULTY MEMBERS

Designing good faculty development programs begins with knowing the interests and capabilities of faculty members and what motivates them. In a survey of faculty participants in the Cultural Legacies project, we asked how much of the material in the core courses lay outside the respondents' area of expertise. The results were astonishing: nearly three-quarters (73 percent) of the respondents said that 50 percent or more of the material was new to them, while nearly one-quarter (22 percent) said 75 percent or more was new material. Yet there was little hesitation or lack of confidence about teaching new courses. This confidence was due in large measure to the prior teaching experience of the faculty members, institutional support for faculty development, and collegial relationships within the program.

Thirty-four percent of the survey respondents were full professors, 27 percent associate professors, 27 percent assistant professors, and 11 percent lecturers (mostly in writing programs). One-third had been teaching at the college level for more than twenty years, 71 percent for more than ten years. The faculty members thus represent a tremendous amount of teaching experience. Some brought new ideas from other institutions and new perspectives from their more recent training, while others were imbued in their campus culture: 35 percent had been teaching at their current institution for five years or fewer and 35 percent sixteen years or more.

In both surveys and on-site interviews, we asked faculty members about their motivations for developing and teaching these new courses. Their responses reveal a group of resourceful and dedicated individuals eager to participate in curricular initiatives that they perceive to be of benefit to students, the institution, and their own renewal. On some campuses, faculty members teaching core courses had little choice; they had been hired with expectations that they teach in the core, or their department chairs requested that they do so. On these and other campuses, however, faculty members were drawn to participate in core programs because of their interest in or commitment to interdisciplinary approaches; their expertise or interest in the new cultures taught in the core; their confidence in the value of the study of primary texts; their belief in the integrity of the program and its goals for student learning; or their desire to participate in a program that promised to contribute to the quality of the institution and to its future direction. Many were swayed by the contagious enthusiasm of the program leaders. Some felt a sense of challenge; others noted their own idealism; still others, the excitement of curricular change.

Faculty members with more recent doctoral training were eager to share perspectives informed by new epistemologies and new approaches to critical analysis and were pleased to learn that these perspectives were viewed as central to the reform of core curricula. They also were eager to interact with colleagues outside their departments and honored to have been referred to program leaders by their department chairs or other colleagues.

The majority, however, made the decision to teach in the core program at least partially because of the opportunity to discuss teaching and engage in intellectually stimulating seminars with colleagues from across campus. The reading lists of the new courses in the Cultural Legacies project contain many classic texts that some faculty members had not read since their own undergraduate years—or perhaps had never read. The opportunity to read these texts alongside texts from cultures that many faculty members yearn to explore proved compelling. These courses tapped into a desire on the part of faculty members who had become specialists to renew their own "general education."

CHOOSING INCENTIVES

We also asked faculty members what incentives helped them decide to participate. The opportunity to interact with colleagues (mentioned by 40 percent) figured almost as prominently as stipends, course reassigned time, and other monetary incentives (mentioned by 50 percent). Merritt Moseley, former director of the Humanities Program at the University of North Carolina–Asheville, refers to this incentive as the "joy of collaboration":

> In a department…we teach our own separate courses; we run along parallel tracks. In an interdisciplinary course like our Humanities, there are ten or fifteen of us teaching roughly the same thing, all of us struggling to do justice to it, meeting on a regular basis to talk about ideas and ways of teaching….
>
> And this collaboration in teaching, and preparing for teaching, can carry over into scholarship. A colleague in Economics and I

[from English] have recently co-authored an essay. It wasn't on any topic we teach together, but the grounds for cooperation, the discussions which led to it, came out of our joint participation in our Humanities course.[34]

Other important incentives were administrative support and encouragement (23 percent) and the desire to improve the curriculum (23 percent). Almost all of the respondents mentioned more than one factor, as in these comments: "In the beginning, I believe there was a stipend.... But the concept of working with other faculty to develop a stimulating new humanities program was the incentive that won my participation"; or, "Presidential support and $$$."

The lesson for curriculum planners is that both types of incentives must be present: the motivating incentives (community, quality curriculum, institutional mission) and the enabling incentives (time and resources for developing and preparing to teach courses). Clearly, faculty members will not participate in a program they believe lacks integrity and substance (unless "ordered" to). Nor can they be expected to sustain enthusiasm or commitment if resources are missing and new course planning competes with other professional obligations for which they gain more visible and concrete institutional rewards.

DESIGNING PROGRAMS

Programs intended to prepare faculty members to teach in new core programs as complex as those in the Cultural Legacies project must be comprehensive. In addition to preparing to teach new content, faculty members must spend time developing new teaching techniques and coordinating their work with colleagues. Wise program leaders scheduled appropriate faculty development activities for each phase of the core development process: planning and course design, core implementation, and ongoing program development. Different activities are needed during each phase of the process.

Planning phase. Successful programs provided resources during the planning stages such as reassigned time for committee chairs, travel monies for faculty members to attend national meetings or visit other campuses, outside consultants, and research and clerical support. Team-building activities were especially important in the early phases of planning, to create common experiences and understanding of the issues to be addressed and the problems to be solved.

Visits to other campuses in the Cultural Legacies project—funded by the NEH grant to AAC—were very helpful for committee members to get information about how core programs work at comparable institutions. Seeing how other institutions respond to questions of structure, content and pedagogy, and resource constraints was extremely helpful. Project participants also profited from visits to their institutions by designated AAC consultants. These consultants interviewed committee members, administrators, faculty members, and students; they clarified plans, identified strengths and weaknesses, provided feedback to planners from the larger campus community, and provided a "reality check" for those immersed in the local process of change. Campuses developing core programs would benefit from building these kinds of faculty development activities into the design phase of their programs.

Course development and piloting. Once faculty members have agreed on a design, the course development phase is the most extensive and hence the most costly in both time and money. Faculty development activities at this stage may make or break implementation of the program because they build the knowledge and skill of the faculty members who will staff the program.

The majority of the institutions in the Cultural Legacies project sequenced these faculty development activities over two to three years, concentrating on either one course at a time or one new cultural heritage that was to be studied in a comparative Western or World Studies course. Most offered intensive summer institutes (two to four weeks) to acquaint faculty members with new materials. In these institutes, faculty members read and discussed texts, listened to lectures by colleagues and outside experts, and discussed and practiced interdisciplinary teaching approaches, and learned new teaching techniques.

These summer programs drew in new faculty members each year, so that the overall program staff was developed sequentially. For the most part, they were funded by outside sources such as the National Endowment for the Humanities, the Fund for the Improvement of Postsecondary Education, Title III grants, state grants for curriculum development, or locally or regionally based private foundations. In many cases, the expenses were borne by the institution and served as a clear indication of the commitment of the administration to the program. Many campuses benefited from the existence of offices or programs for faculty development that regularly hold seminars in the summer or during term breaks. Those core programs that had been in effect for some years and were making changes used their regularly scheduled seminars to do faculty development.

A seminar at Brandeis University serves as a good example. With support from the Ford Foundation, Brandeis offered "Increasing Diversity on Campus: The Integration of Africa-Based Texts Into the Humanities Core Curriculum" (see page 71), a four-week summer faculty development seminar for twenty-four faculty members interested in incorporating new texts into their core courses. In addition to meeting three hours per day to discuss texts and teaching approaches, faculty members had daily reading, writing assignments, and two or three special events per week such as films, guest lectures, or text readings by authors.

Other campuses accomplished the same goals by running a series of workshops or seminars during the year prior to course implementation and providing a stipend or released time for faculty participation, or a combination of both. Carthage College holds regular retreats and symposia for faculty members teaching in the Heritage Studies program. Many of these activities focus specifically on pedagogy, and outside consultants are invited to address goals, strategies, and needs for teaching writing, communication, and critical thinking across the four Heritage seminars.

Other programs paid for group or individual study abroad or used visiting scholars as a resource for faculty development. The University of Richmond, for example, brought in a Fulbright Visiting Scholar from Egypt to participate in a seminar designed to acquaint core faculty members with Middle Eastern texts, make classroom presentations, and give several public talks.

The length and intensity of faculty development programs will vary directly in relation to the amount of new material and pedagogical techniques the faculty members are expected to learn. Faculty development program costs for institutions in the Cultural Legacies project—which were as large as $75,000 per year—were well justified because the seminars and workshops created a core group of fifteen to twenty-five faculty members who had the interest, motivation, and competence to teach in the program.

Reassigned time is equally important during the piloting of courses, especially where commonality across multiple sections is a goal and core faculty members function as a team. These instructors rely on weekly or biweekly meetings to discuss with each other how to frame the texts or topics, which concepts are essential to highlight, areas in which students are likely to experience difficulty, and good teaching techniques. Consultation outside these meetings also is very common.

Faculty participants in the Cultural Legacies project, when asked how they gained the knowledge needed to teach the new courses, most

BRANDEIS UNIVERSITY
HUMANITIES FACULTY DEVELOPMENT SEMINAR
JUNE 1991
READING LIST BY WEEK

**Pre-Seminar
Reading:** Giles Gunn, *The Culture of Criticism and the Criticism of Culture*

Week One: *Mwindo*, trans. Biebuyck & Mateene
Sundiata, trans. Niane
packets:
1) poems & songs
2) theory: Luria, Svenbro, Vygotsky, Nagy, Ong, Havelock, Lord

Week Two: Apuleius, *The Golden Ass*
Marcel Griaule, *Conversations with Ogoutemeli*
Chinua Achebe, *Things Fall Apart*
Okot p'Bitek, *The Song of Lawino & the Song of Ocol*
Julius Lester, *Lovesong*
Zora Neale Hurston, *Moses, Man of the Mountain*
Gilgamesh, trans. Kovacs
Ousmane Sembene, *God's Bits of Wood*
Buchi Emecheta, *The Joys of Motherhood*
A. Kourouma, *Sons of Independence*
Chinua Achebe, *Anthills of the Savannah*
packets:
1) selections *De Iside*, iconography, Bernal, Eliade
2) mysteries and commentaries: neoplatonic, psychoanalytic, Jungian
3) Frances Ellen Watkins Harper, "Moses, a Story of the Nile"; Charles Chesnutt, "The Fall of Adam"

Week Three: Robert Thompson, *Flash of the Spirit*
Joel Chandler Harris, *Uncle Remus*
Zora Neale Hurston, *Of Mules and Men*
Jay Wright, *The Double Invention of Como*
Frederick Douglass, *Narrative of the Life of Frederick Douglass*
packets:
1) "Been In the Storm Too Long," Folkways (record); "Negro Work Songs and Calls," Folk Music of the United States, Library of Congress
2) "Fear of a Black Planet," Public Enemy (record)

Week Four: Ralph Ellison, *Invisible Man*
Ishmael Reed, *Mumbo Jumbo*

often responded that they read the material and then sought out knowl-
edgeable colleagues to assist them in interpretation. "We learned from each
other" was a frequent comment. On dozens of campuses, the development
of core programs has motivated faculty members to talk to each other in
substantive ways across departmental boundaries, creating community
among the faculty.

Core program leaders' expectations were not that faculty members
gain the same level of expertise that they possessed in their own fields but
that they possess the willingness to participate in designing rich intellectual experiences for students exploring cultural pluralism. Still, some faculty members were justifiably leery of stepping outside the boundaries of
their specialties, especially in arenas such as core programs that made their
teaching more visible to their colleagues. Faculty members at several institutions noted that they had been hesitant about joining the program until
they realized how much assistance they would have from colleagues and
from well-structured faculty development activities. They especially praised
activities that taught them methods for initiating discussion, clarifying students' ideas, and helping students analyze texts and their contexts.

The development and piloting phases are excellent times to
involve students in the process, although few of the institutions in the
Cultural Legacies project used this strategy. We saw in Chapter 2 how graduate students in the English Department at Washington State University
assisted in the development of a core reader for the writing course linked to
the World Civilizations core course. The development of the Crossroads
program at the University of Wyoming was facilitated by a graduate-level
seminar in the humanities in which senior honors students, graduate students, and faculty members worked together to develop various segments of
the course. Involving graduate students—especially those preparing to
teach in higher education—in core faculty development activities not only
benefits the institution but also helps to guarantee that colleges and universities will have a pool of faculty members who have experience teaching
interdisciplinary core courses.

The conclusion of the pilot phase is the time to begin faculty
development activities that lay the groundwork for implementing and sustaining the program. At the end of the three-year pilot phase at Tufts
University, all of the instructors who had taught in the three core
sequences came together for a three-week summer workshop (included in
the grant funds they had received from NEH) and for an additional week in
the fall. They assessed what had been accomplished in the courses, pre-

pared a five-year phase-in budget, and developed information to submit to the faculty as a whole to aid in the approval process for the new core. The documents that emerged from the summer workshop included revised course syllabi, a series of operating guidelines for the program, and an overview of the program that included reviews from external evaluators. In addition, those who had already taught the course conducted a two-day workshop designed to introduce other interested faculty members to the concept and practice of teaching core courses.

Sustaining the program. During the initial years of a new program, faculty enthusiasm and energy run high. There is the excitement of creation and experimentation and the pleasure of being associated with a group of colleagues testing new ideas about teaching. After several years, however, core programs face the challenge of sustaining enthusiasm and energy. One particular difficulty many programs face is recruiting new faculty members to the program when the major faculty development programs are over.

The University of North Carolina–Asheville has created a very successful faculty development program designed to sustain its core curriculum. The four-semester interdisciplinary humanities sequence has operated for more than a quarter of a century; it engages 2,600 undergraduates annually in reading major texts primarily, but not solely, from Western traditions. In any given year, faculty members teaching in the core represent 60 to 70 percent of the twenty UNCA departments. To sustain the quality of the courses and prepare new faculty members to teach in them, UNCA provides an internship program.

Faculty members in this program receive reassigned time for working with a colleague who is experienced in the course they plan to teach, for sitting in on their mentor's course and others, and for reading background material for the course. Both new and experienced faculty members meet weekly to clarify sequencing, discuss content and goals for the course, prepare for upcoming subject matter, and share ideas about readings, teaching methods, and interdisciplinary approaches. Occasionally, with the assistance of outside funds, special seminars or workshops are conducted to invigorate the core faculty and prepare them to make revisions in the texts or cultures taught in the core. Fairleigh Dickinson University—which also has a four-course core sequence with a different faculty teaching team for each—has replicated this internship program; several other institutions in the Cultural Legacies project also are experimenting with internships.

Other kinds of faculty development activities help create a culture that supports the core as the intellectual center of the curriculum and the campus. Guest speakers, distinguished lecture series, visiting scholars, festivals, student research conferences, newsletters, journals, or programs on the campus radio station help set a tone for the academic life of the campus. These kinds of activities also enhance the core program by bringing faculty members, students, and staff members together around central areas of teaching and scholarship.

BENEFITS FOR FACULTY MEMBERS

Good faculty development has enormous benefits. Jerry Gaff describes participation in a process of curriculum reform as "a means of restoring wholeness in faculty life." [35] Some faculty members found a level of acceptance, respect, encouragement, and collegial engagement among the core faculty that they had never felt in their own departments. One faculty member offered a telling story: After years of successful teaching in his department, he had been marginalized by a new department chair because he lacked a terminal degree; yet he had participated successfully in faculty development activities for the core and had become a valued peer and intellectual leader of the program. Given this external recognition, the chair rethought his evaluation of the faculty member.

The most successful programs develop and maintain this sense of community among faculty members, who are "learners together." While constituted of able and well-grounded faculty members from traditional "core" humanities disciplines, the core program is not viewed either as an elite group of outstanding teacher/ scholars, nor as a dumping ground for faculty members whose courses don't contribute substantially to the departmental curriculum. David Leary, dean of arts and sciences at the University of Richmond, notes that the key to success is "playing the game with the faculty you've got": recognizing their strengths and limitations and creating an environment that ensures they will all flourish.

Many faculty members and administrators also noted the impact of interdisciplinary teaching on faculty research productivity: Many took a new focus on their area of expertise, some started doing comparative studies, others made contributions to the pedagogy in their field. Their enthusiasm for new insights they gained from teaching in the core carried over into their scholarship.

THE HAZARDS OF INADEQUATE FACULTY PREPARATION

As with any curricular initiative, inadequate faculty preparation in either
content or pedagogy results in core curricula that look good on paper but
do not deliver what they promise. When rhetoric outdistances reality,
faculty members and students become cynical, frustrated, and even angry.
Overly ambitious expectations for teaching diverse cultural traditions can
contribute to failure.

In a few cases, we observed faculty members teaching topics in
which they clearly were not well-grounded and with which they were
visibly uncomfortable.[36] Some of the strategies used to compensate for
their limited knowledge base were problematic. In some instances, faculty
members were recycling concepts and organizing principles from their own
fields of specialty as a way of managing new course content with which
they were ill-at-ease. This approach filled up the class hour but not in ways
that advanced course goals. In other instances, faculty members relied
heavily on student presentations in what seemed inappropriate ways. Some
students presented content central to a course as personal testimony rather
than as interpretation, argument, or analysis. The instructors might have
established a context in which such testimony became the basis for dialogue and discussion; in fact, they had not. The students asserted; the class
took notes; and positions most scholars would question were not explored.

There also were some instances in which students tended to
assume they knew more than they did about a culture they had encountered through one text only. One way we learn is to assimilate unfamiliar
information into patterns and experiences with which we are familiar. For
different cultural manifestations, this approach is dangerous, especially if it
oversimplifies contexts and fails to emphasize the careful analysis of texts
and the meaning of difference. Successful core programs set up structures
that allowed faculty members to rely on each other's expertise—in effect,
to intern—while acquiring the necessary depth of understanding to teach
unfamiliar texts and contexts.

GOOD PRACTICE IN FACULTY DEVELOPMENT PROGRAMS

Luckily for our new assistant professor of Japanese history—who did decide to teach in the core program—Old Ivy College had determined at the outset of planning for a new core curriculum that faculty development was essential. Program leaders planned an extensive program of activities and were careful to:

- design a high-quality program of faculty development with the collaboration of faculty members themselves at the start of the planning process

- examine programs that have worked well on campuses with similar curricular plans

- assess the developmental needs of faculty members

- set clear expectations for faculty participation and outcomes in each stage of the process

- design specific activities for the planning, pilot, implementation, and assessment phases of the program

- include both theoretical and practical components in the program

- use the expertise available among faculty members at the institution as well as outside experts

- design the scope and intensity of activities according to the expectations placed on faculty members

- provide enough resources to compensate faculty members for the amount and kind of work expected of them.

4 Implementing Programs

▶ An institution can't import a core program: a successful program fits the local context, reflects the institutional mission and vision of the faculty, and meets student needs.

▶ Core design and implementation is a three- to five-year process. Along the way, there are mazes, bogs, potholes, vistas, forked roads, dead ends, and watering holes. There are no short-cuts.

▶ The process is as important as the product; a good planning and implementation process improves chances for success.

Within two months of its acceptance into the Cultural Legacies project, the core curriculum proposal at one of the most highly-rated applicant institutions was dead. An innovative and imaginative design for a four-semester sequence of courses, the proposal proved to be the vision of a small group of faculty members who worked apart from their colleagues in preparing it. Although there was strong administrative backing for the proposal, this support was not sufficient to carry the proposal to fruition. Ultimately, the administration could not support the views of a handful of faculty members against the larger faculty community.

At another institution, the faculty senate voted down a carefully prepared core proposal that had been two years in the planning and that the majority of the faculty supported. The president and several academic administrators came to the faculty senate to exercise their right to vote on the proposal; their presence alienated the faculty, who saw this move as an effort to railroad the proposal.

Curriculum change is a political process. Defining or changing core studies involves negotiations among all sectors of the campus that have vested interests. While many institutional cultures do not value teaching within the core or general education to the same degree they value teaching in the disciplines, most faculty members in the liberal arts have an unshakable belief that their field is essential to core studies. Engaging the multiplicity of cultures within the core brings an additional layer of politically contested decisions to an already turbulent process.

By the end of the two-year Cultural Legacies project, most of the participating institutions—having reached faculty consensus about the configuration of core studies, at least at one time during their participation—were at the stage of piloting and evaluating new core courses. Their design and piloting processes had taken at least three years. (Most had spent time on program planning before applying to the AAC project.) Implementation processes at institutions that were further along took another two to three years.

Any institution embarking on the reform of core studies must realize that this is a long-term process that will have ups and downs, starts and stalls. Many of these fluctuations will come from faculty and administrative turnover during the process. Institutional commitment to an effective planning and implementation process, therefore, is essential from the outset. It is this process that will ensure benefits for students, faculty members, and the institution—even if the initial "core package" is voted down or sent back to the drawing board for revision.

ARTICULATING A VISION FOR CHANGE

The first step of the core design process is to develop a vision of how the new core will benefit the students, the institution, and the faculty. This vision will become embedded in the design for the new core. The vision must fit the institution's culture, as it is or as it is evolving, and it must draw upon institutional strengths and enhance the institution's unique niche in higher education. It is important to involve all sectors of the campus community—the board, students, faculty, staff, and graduates. Attaching the vision to an institutional milestone, such as a centennial celebration or the advent of the twenty-first century, can add weight to undertaking a review and preparing for change.

In the majority of institutions participating in the Cultural Legacies project, a new president, academic vice president, or dean provided the impetus for renewal of the institution's commitment to liberal learning as reflected in the creation or restoration of some version of core studies. The new administrator's vision for and prior experience with curriculum change may have been a central factor in the hiring process, so that she or he comes to the institution with a mandate—implicit or explicit—for initiating such change. The institution may have been facing a changing student profile, enrollment problems, or any number of issues that increased curricular coherence and vitality would help address. In situations like these, it becomes the new administrator's challenge to inspire and encourage the faculty to take up and own the task of reform.

On other campuses, core curriculum reform was a grass roots effort emerging from a regular review of the general-education program or through the interests of a group of faculty members in bringing about change. The faculty leaders' role, in this case, is to secure the support of the administration and other faculty members. Basing the reform in previously articulated consensus about the need for improvement or change is a good way to begin.

We saw in Chapter 1 the typical problems that faculty members cite in urging new curricular initiatives: lack of coherence, lack of integration of learning, lack of adequate attention to skills development, lack of depth of study, and a need to update the curriculum in light of current scholarship, especially in the realm of cultural pluralism. Such appeals are most effective when they are backed by evidence; faculty advocates for creating or restorating a liberal arts core often will need to support the case they are making to skeptical or overburdened colleagues.

A major pitfall at the beginning of the process is failure to develop a rationale for change that is conceptually and intellectually sound and grounded in an appropriate philosophy of undergraduate education and an analysis of student needs. Core planning processes at several institutions in the Cultural Legacies project stalled because the reason for change was purely logistical, such as compensating for shifts in student enrollment patterns or reducing faculty teaching loads. These kinds of issues can be dealt with during program implementation; they do not serve well as the primary reason for change.

Another common pitfall is gearing program design to a specific grant competition. Elaine Maimon of CUNY–Queens College argues persuasively, "Only write a grant proposal if the project will be done whatever happens. Treat the awarding of the grant as serendipity, not as the driving force and reason for action."[37]

Finally, setting goals that are too short-sighted limits one's vision of what might be. Some planners relied too heavily on the expertise of the current faculty in designing programs. It would serve institutions well, as one consultant noted, to think beyond the current institutional "fit" between the core and the faculty and ask, "Where do we want to be in twenty years?"

BUILDING A COLLABORATIVE PLANNING PROCESS

While the impetus for undertaking change at a particular moment in an institution's history may be either "top-down" or "grass roots," it is impossible to implement a program of core studies without the collaboration of faculty members and the administration. Establishing and maintaining equilibrium between administrative support and faculty ownership of new programs is a key factor for the ultimate success of the initiative. Both faculty and administrative perspectives and leadership are necessary to create a dynamic and high-quality core curriculum.

Faculty planners and administrators must think strategically about their roles in the development of new programs. Faculty members—within whose purview the curriculum falls—bring to the process their knowledge of fields and their credibility as scholars and teachers. As teachers, they have insight into the needs, interests, and characteristics of students. Faculty leaders know the history of the institution from the perspective of departments and programs and can identify the various cultures operating within different units that will have an impact on the shape of core requirements. They must be willing not just to design the new curriculum but to speak for it—to design courses and teach them. They must be citizens of the institution, supporting balance and coherence in curricula and extracurricular activities.

Administrators have the ability to focus attention on curricular reform, identify resources, and clarify the purposes of curricular initiatives in relation to institutional missions and goals. Through the judicious use of symbolic and real resources, good administrators can make it clear that core reform is an important priority—and why it is important. They must not, however, try to force their vision of a program on others. When constituting committees or task forces, they should select faculty members in whom they and others have confidence and then actively support and advance the committee's work. They must not allow committee planning to continue in isolation from larger faculty dialogue, however. They need to work hard to keep the community informed and to answer key questions, and they should use their positions to facilitate the decision-making process by negotiating outcomes and structures that benefit departments and faculty members who contribute to core programs. Finally, they must show that they fully support implementation of the program.

The design committee. The composition of the core design committee can make or break the initiative. Deciding whom to involve may differ according to the campus culture, governance structure, union power, or other factors. In most programs in the Cultural Legacies project, the committee was appointed by the administrator overseeing the effort—the dean of arts and sciences or the vice president for academic affairs—in consultation with the faculty, department chairs, or established curriculum committees.

Most of the successful programs created a new task force or committee to design the core program so that the committee would not bring the "baggage" of established modes of interaction and prior discussions or reforms to the table. However, it is essential to define the role of this design group in relation to established governance structures so that the process will not be perceived as breaking from established procedures of curriculum change at the institution.

Above all, design committees need individuals who have credibility with their colleagues: campus opinion leaders who are identified by their knowledge of the institution; their insight into national trends; and their reputations as good teachers, good scholars, and good citizens of the campus. The committee also must include individuals with specific expertise in areas that are central to the proposed reform, such as Western civilization, world cultures, U.S. pluralism, interdisciplinary studies, and the arts. Many core planners in the Cultural Legacies project remarked on the importance of capitalizing on the knowledge and experience of those in writing programs, faculty development programs, area studies, women's studies, and American ethnic studies. Others made effective use of faculty members with backgrounds in science and society.

A good committee will have visionaries and pragmatists, risk-takers and conservatives, problem-identifiers and problem-solvers. It will not be composed of people reflecting a single intellectual, cultural, gender, or generational perspective. Student representation—while conspicuously absent in most Cultural Legacies core planning committees—adds another important voice to the discussions and helps establish the credibility of the new curriculum with students as well as with faculty members.

Those who are elected or selected should have interest in the task and time to devote to the process. One of the pitfalls in committee selection is using people who are so overcommitted that they cannot make room for the work of the committee. It is bad for committee morale to include "tokens"—those who bring credibility but who cannot devote any real time or attention to the effort. In cases where these kinds of leaders are necessary, a larger, representative group can be convened, with smaller tasks groups that develop proposals to present to this larger group.

Effective committees start their deliberations by providing opportunities for members to learn about one another, what they each bring to the process, and what concerns they have. Attention to the process within the committee helps individual committee members feel they have a voice and are part of a team. Team-building activities such as seminars, visits to other campuses, and travel to professional meetings help solidify commitment to the process.

At the outset, the committee should have a clear sense of its charge and the scope of its responsibility. The charge might include assessment of need; review of the curriculum in place; identification of strengths; discussion of possible models from other institutions; review of national trends, reports, and resources; provision of information and solicitation of input from the campus community at important junctures; and identification of the resources necessary to the scope of change contemplated. The committee should establish how it will interact with the administration and with other faculty or curriculum committees. It should carefully plan a campus communication strategy.

Committee members should assign responsibility for specific tasks and establish a time line for accomplishing them. At this point, a request for resources for the design phase is appropriate. It is advisable to assign at least a half-time salary or released time for the person who chairs the committee. Funds are needed for assessment, visits to other campuses, travel to professional meetings, and faculty development, if the program is to be based in the best of current practice. Dividing the process into analysis, design, pilot, and implementation phases ensures careful planning. On most campuses in the Cultural Legacies project, a second committee— composed almost entirely of faculty members teaching the courses—was formed to pilot and implement the program.

ASSESSING THE CLIMATE FOR CHANGE

Those who lead curricular change efforts of any kind must be or become very familiar with the organizational culture. Core program planners must understand the politics of change on the campus and assess carefully those factors that will enhance the likelihood of success, as well as those that might derail the initiative. The challenges of engaging cultural pluralism, particularly in interdisciplinary core curricula, bring into play several institutional areas of change: the institution; the curriculum as a whole; the faculty; the students; individual courses; and teaching practices. The degree of "readiness" of each area plays an important role in the change process and must be taken into account by core planners. An excellent starting place for the committee charged with designing the core is to make a systematic assessment of each area. Questions might include:

Institution

- What parts of the institutional mission statement support reform of the core curriculum?

- What are the meanings of "core curriculum" at this institution? Will core mean common course of study or general-education requirements?

- What are the institutional motivations for undertaking reform of the core curriculum at this time?

- Is this institutional intent widely understood?

- How much support is there in the administration?

- What resources and networks can the institution make use of for this effort?

- What messages has the administration conveyed regarding curriculum and cultural pluralism at the institution?

Students

- What are the characteristics of the current student body?

- Has this profile changed substantially in the last decade?

- Will it change considerably in the next ten to fifteen years?

- What educational needs have the students articulated?

- What educational needs has the educational community identified for students?

- How well does the current core curriculum serve students? How do we know?

Curriculum

- What are the strengths and deficiencies of the current general-education or core curriculum?

- What is the history of reform of the core curriculum? What parts of the collective institutional memory of previous reforms will play a role in this reform ("We tried that before and it didn't work"; "We've voted down three core proposals in the past five years!")?

- What kinds of core curricula have been successful at institutions like ours?

- What special commitments of the institution should be reflected in the core curriculum?

- How do we currently define core curriculum? Is this definition a good one?

- How much commonality can the institution sustain in the core?

Faculty

- What is the nature and degree of faculty support for the existing general-education/core program?

- What is the understanding among faculty members about the necessity of engaging cultural pluralism in the curriculum?

- How much do faculty members value the following: a common experience for all students? active involvement of students in core programs? skills development in core programs? interdisciplinary humanities approaches? involvement of faculty members from different fields in the core? connections between and among courses?

- What expertise in the area of cultural pluralism exists among the faculty at present?

- What incentives will appeal to faculty members?

- Who is likely support change? to resist change?

Courses

- Are there courses that already exist that engage students in common learning? What are their goals? What approaches do they use? How effective are they?

- Which courses already attend to cultural pluralism? What are their goals? What approaches do they use? How effective are they?

Pedagogy

- What kinds of training have faculty members received in different pedagogies, such as writing across the curriculum, media-assisted teaching, collaborative learning, interdisciplinary teaching?

- What kinds of teaching do faculty members value?

- What kinds of teaching should be central to the core?

- Do we have a sufficient cadre of faculty members to teach integrative courses in history, culture, and the arts? To help students interpret primary materials from different cultures?

By answering questions like these, the committee can identify institutional strengths as well as barriers to change. These questions also can pinpoint areas of consensus and disagreement that may mirror those in the faculty at large. If the committee is to present a clear rationale for change to the faculty as a whole, it will first have to work toward consensus among its members (see "Gaining Support for the Program" below).

Core design committees have used a variety of methods to assess the climate for change. These include: surveying faculty members about their views on core; reviewing student transcripts; interviewing students about their goals and the degree to which the curriculum is meeting them; holding focus groups for students and for faculty members; and reviewing institutional documents such as accreditation reviews, curriculum committee reports, and data on student success.

The committee will have to pay careful attention to messages about the need or prospects for change that have already been sent, both explicitly and implicitly, to the campus community. Early in the process, the design committee should seek input from the faculty about general directions for the new core. Answers to the assessment questions are best developed with as much input as possible or practical.

GAINING SUPPORT FOR THE PROGRAM

The design phase requires an extraordinary amount of faculty collaboration. This is the part of the process in which choices from among many core configurations will have to be narrowed down to one model or variations on a central model. The stakes are high, as the faculty wrestles with making choices about content and pedagogy. The various arts and sciences departments will advocate for their own beliefs and interests, and all units of the institution whose students will be affected by the new program will hold strong opinions. At this juncture, clear educational goals are essential since they can be used to evaluate competing alternatives.

During this phase of the work, there should be a clear delineation of roles, responsibility, and authority. A core proposal may fail because the design committee assumes it has more power than it does and fails to communicate with appropriate administrators and faculty governance bodies at times when they are making key decisions. On the other hand, the committee can become overwhelmed with input, or too much political maneuvering outside of the committee, if it shares too much of its deliberations before clear ideas of possible models emerge. Planners need to have some sense of what the faculty is likely (or unlikely) to support. It is essential,

however, that the planners and the administration agree about the goals of
the program before going public.

Once the core planners and administrators, including department
chairs, are in general agreement about the purpose and design of the core,
the committee can engage the faculty at large in the discussions. John
Thorpe, vice provost and dean of the Undergraduate College at SUNY–
Buffalo, suggests that a successful process of building consensus about a curriculum proposal will involve a feedback loop:[38]

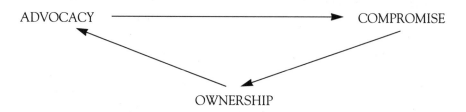

ADVOCACY   COMPROMISE

OWNERSHIP

The original designers of the proposal become advocates for its
adoption to a larger group (perhaps a curriculum committee or a subcommittee of the faculty senate). This results in a dialogue in which many of
the concerns of the larger group are resolved and some lead to modifications in the proposal (compromise). In helping to shape the proposal, the
members of the larger group take ownership of it and join the advocacy
group as the proposal moves to a larger forum. The process continues until
the body with authority to approve the proposal has taken ownership.

If the core committee is appropriately representative, most of the
positions that emerge from the faculty at large will have surfaced in the pre-
liminary discussions of the committee. Reaching out to the campus community at the start of the process is essential. This should be done in systematic
and comprehensive ways. One-on-one conversations with colleagues are
important, as is discussion in departments and programs. Presentations to
the whole faculty are equally critical, so that there are forums in which
everybody is hearing the same information at the same time. It is in these
kinds of sessions that the give-and-take between the design committee and
the general faculty allows for the kind of consensus-building that will yield a
successful proposal. This also is the setting in which counter-proposals will
surface that will have to be taken into account.

The faculty-administrative alliance often is put to the test at this
juncture. It may be hard for administrators to resist the temptation of advo-
cating a specific proposal, particularly the one emerging from "their" committee. Overwhelmingly, core directors and planners of successful programs

in the Cultural Legacies project remarked that a key element in their success was the "hands-off" manner of the dean or vice president. These key administrators publicly supported the importance of reform, reiterated their trust in the committee and confidence in the faculty, provided resources, negotiated logistical and political problems, and allowed the faculty to do their work. Good administrators also helped the design committee keep perspective. "I kept reminding them," remarks David Leary, dean of Arts and Sciences at the University of Richmond, "that our goal was excellence, not perfection."

In every case where the process worked, large numbers of faculty members were consulted or officially involved in some capacity. At LeMoyne-Owen College, for example, 75 percent of the faculty members were involved in developing or teaching the core. At some campuses, design committees created subcommittees for specific tasks in order to create a sense of ownership among a larger number of faculty members. In most cases, by the time a proposal came to a vote, the committee had consulted widely with the various constituencies.

Faculty development activities at the planning stage are a good way to involve the larger campus community in discussion of the design of the program, especially when there are divisions of opinion about the best route to take. Outside speakers can be helpful at these programs in bringing a national perspective to bear on local concerns. The "Core Convo" organized at Oglethorpe University (see pages 88–89) is an excellent example of such a program.

ANTICIPATING PROBLEMS AND RESISTANCES

While there are numerous unforeseen problems or events that can cause planning processes to stall or fail, many problems and resistances are predictable. If anticipated, their effects can be minimized through carefully thought-out processes that reflect and respect institutional procedures and faculty goodwill and integrity.

Resistance to change. Gaining the academic credentials necessary for a teaching position in higher education requires years of training; keeping up with current research in one's field in order to be effective in the classroom and in the profession requires continuing investments of time, energy, and support. Because success depends, in large measure, on specialization, faculty members' identities are tightly intertwined with their

OGLETHORPE UNIVERSITY
CORE CONVO

September 17, 1991
10:30 AM   Opening session
            "Important Considerations for Forming a Core"—Thomas Flynn,
            Dean of the College, Mt. Saint Mary's College, Maryland
            "Core Reform as a Current Issue in Higher Education"—Frank
            Frankfort, Program Officer, NEH
            "Reforming the OU Core Curriculum"—Victoria Weiss,
            Professor of English and Project Director for the institutional
            grant from NEH/AAC to reform the core curriculum at
            Oglethorpe
11:50–12:40 First session of discussion groups (see topics, leaders, and ques-
            tions below)
12:40–1:15 Lunch break
1:15–2:00   Second session of discussion groups (same topics, leaders, and
            questions as first session)

Discussion groups (topics, leaders, and questions to be discussed):
#1   "Important Considerations for Forming a Core"—Thomas Flynn
#2   "Core Reform as a Current Issue in U.S. Higher Education"
      —Frank Frankfort
      What do you think every student ought to know?
#3   "Interdisciplinary and Capstone Courses as Part of a Core Curriculum"
      —Joseph Knippenberg
            Are the questions and problems we encounter as human beings
            each simply the preserve of one academic discipline?
            Should we approach these problems in the course of studying a
            particular discipline, or should we examine them as they present
            themselves in their own terms?
            Assuming that it is inevitable that students "major" in a particular
            field, should they be required to confront the strengths, weaknesses,
            and limitations of the methods and approaches characteristic of
            their discipline late in their academic careers?
            What is a liberally educated person supposed to know? What
            kind of core curriculum is most conducive to the attainment of
            liberal learning?
#4   "Ways of Organizing a Core Curriculum at OU"—Victoria Weiss
            What can be done to ensure that core courses speak to one
            another, that what is studied in one core course can be related to
            what is studied in another core course?
            What can we do to ensure that the core stays vital, that it continues
            to remain clear to both students and professors alike why any
            given course is in the core?
            What can we do to make sure that core courses focus on significant
            ways of knowing rather than on narrow areas of professorial or
            student interest?

89

#5   "Science in General Education and Laboratory Science as a Core Course"
—Michael Rulison
Why should (or shouldn't) there be a science component in a liberal
arts university?
If it is granted that there should be a core science component,
what kind of science experience would be most useful and/or
most stimulating to students pursuing various majors?
The worst thing about science core courses is....
The best thing about science core courses is....
How does a core science course enhance, build on, illuminate,
complement, etc. the other aspects of a core experience?
Resolved: A true science experience must involve a laboratory.
Pros? Cons?

#6   "Areas of Inquiry Addressed by the OU Core"—William Shropshire
When you finish your history assignment and begin work on your
biology, what sort of mental adjustment do you make? Do you
feel like you are doing a different kind of thinking? What is the
difference? How about literature vs. economics? Mathematics vs.
philosophy?
Have you ever felt like you were being creative? Under what
circumstances? While reading? Writing? Doing a lab experiment?
How do you come to accept or reject propositions such as "the
earth is round" or "humans are self-interested"?

#7   "The Politics of Core Reform: Inclusion and Exclusion" —Madeline
Picciotto
How do we determine what every Oglethorpe student should
learn?
Is there a canon of great books that everyone should read, a set of
crucial skills that everyone should master, a series of significant
questions that everyone should explore?
Who decides?
To what extent should students themselves be involved in the
process?

unique knowledge base. Substantive changes to the curriculum that call for new content expertise are extremely threatening. For some, change becomes even more threatening when the central issue is whose culture(s) will be at the core of the curriculum.

Core advocates can begin to address such fears by creating opportunities for dialogue and discussion—forums in which everyone has a chance to state her or his perspective, be heard, hear contrasting perspectives, and either modify those views or recognize that most of the faculty members hold another view. Johnnella Butler has used the term "difficult dialogues" to describe this process of faculty interaction on matters of real consequence for the life of the institution in these contentious times.[39] Many core planners in the Cultural Legacies project noted that presenting colleagues with the intellectual and social rationales for revising the curriculum and directly addressing their concerns was a good beginning. Outside speakers and consultants are a good means to bring these perspectives to the campus. Providing reading materials is effective in encouraging colleagues to investigate new approaches. Faculty members will be more willing to attempt change if they receive clear indications of what they are expected to learn and do, as well as institutional support for their work.

Turf protection. Traditionally, the site of power over the curriculum in higher education has been the academic department, and departmental priorities have not centered on contributions to general education. The organizational culture disperses authority over curricular matters among many separate departments, which have much more power to veto initiatives than to initiate changes that affect other units. The stronger and more autonomous traditional departments are, the more difficulty there will be in gaining collaboration for an interdisciplinary core program in the humanities, especially if these departments contribute discipline-based courses to the present core. Distribution requirements that represent negotiated settlements of the number of credit hours for each major area present formidable barriers to change.

Again, observation of institutional practice is revealing. Some programs in the Cultural Legacies project were stymied by departmental turf protection. Approval processes ground to a halt, as departmental faculties expressed their concerns over how the new core was "weighted" by disciplines. There were instances in which an English or history department—or individual faculty members within it—did not want to relinquish control over a course in world literature or Western civilization. In some cases, the "interdisciplinary" core was created with the absence of one central humanities discipline, and a course requirement in this field was added to the program as a compromise to move the core proposal forward.

In other cases, core reform was taking place in a context of larger change in the institutional culture—occasioned by, for example, the different leadership style of a new president or other administrator. When responsibility for planning is fully delegated to faculty members—especially when the prior administration had been autocratic—turf battles may erupt, as tightly controlled decision making is loosened.

The relationship between the liberal arts and sciences and professional schools also is critical. Professional schools usually will express concern over a new core that adds additional credits to undergraduate requirements. Some institutions have overcome these barriers by offering a minimal liberal arts and sciences core that is required of all undergraduates, while adding more courses for the arts and sciences students. Professional schools may choose on their own to add more liberal arts credits; business, law, engineering, and nursing schools all are coming to the realization that their students need to study cultural pluralism and cross-cultural communications skills if they are to be effective professionals. Coordinating core offerings to make use of the faculty members in these schools who focus on these topics, or on values and ethics, is a good practice.

Administrators must work with core planners to set up structures that reward departments for their contributions to the core. John Pierce, dean of the Division of Humanities and Social Sciences in the College of Sciences and Arts at Washington State University, created strategies—such as adding graduate teaching assistants—to enhance departments that contributed heavily to the core. An evaluation of program results showed that central departments made strong contributions to the core at the same time they enhanced their research productivity. Variations on this approach were used in several large universities to win departmental support for a core program.

Overburdening the core course(s): issues of coverage. Nearly all of the institutions in the Cultural Legacies project dealt with the issue of placing too many expectations on the core course or courses. One of the pitfalls was the temptation to add new cultures to existing Western civilization courses while still attempting to teach a tremendous amount of the old syllabus. In some cases, not only was significant new content added, but the course also added perspectives from a variety of disciplines and adopted collaborative learning activities. There is only so much that one course can do. By and large, those institutions that developed sequences of courses and linked courses were better able than those with one core course to address a full range of educational goals.

Core planners in the Cultural Legacies project dealt with colleagues' concerns about coverage by emphasizing that concentration on a manageable number of significant texts, concepts, and skills in a course was preferable to coverage of the whole sweep of history and culture from the ancients to the present. These choices are difficult ones and perhaps are best addressed by setting up a sequence of courses to address different goals that the faculty enunciates for core study. Core study then can be complemented by a range of other courses students take in general education, the major, or as electives.

Reward systems. Core planners also have to contend with the traditional institutional structures through which rewards are channeled. In those institutions in which colleges and academic departments are strong and largely autonomous, in which administration is decentralized, and in which there is little collaboration across these boundaries, there is little incentive for faculty members to participate in programs that pull them out of their departmental structure.

SUNY–Buffalo found a good solution to this dilemma that served as a first step to developing a core curriculum. In 1986—three years before the Cultural Legacies project began—the university had created an Undergraduate College in which fifty senior faculty members develop and teach core courses. These faculty members remain in their academic departments but commit a substantial portion of their time and energy to the general-education curriculum for a three-year, renewable term. Thus, the new unit parallels traditional ones in the university. The college is respected because of the quality of the faculty members associated with it.

One of the first challenges that faculty members raise to those who seek to involve them extensively in planning or teaching in the core will be: How can I be sure I won't be penalized for my involvement? No matter how much support there is from the administration, if this support does not translate into merit considerations, faculty members will rightly hesitate to become involved. This question is particularly troublesome for junior faculty members. Core directors in the Cultural Legacies project who argued strongly for the participation of junior faculty members in core programs also ensured through discussions with appropriate administrators and with the faculty members themselves that they would not be penalized at tenure and promotion for their involvement.

Ideally, the core reform process should go hand in hand with evaluation of the reward structure: promotion and tenure guidelines, faculty development opportunities, leaves, and so forth. Yet it was clear in this project that changes in the reward structure are lagging far behind new expectations being placed on faculty members. Institutions large and small had not come to terms with what it means to form a faculty that is prepared, charged, and rewarded for their contributions to liberal arts core curricula. Until institutions structure themselves in ways that reward faculty members and departments for contributions to all of the educational goals of the institution, departmental power will pose problems for general education and for core programs.

MAKING GOOD USE OF THE PILOT PERIOD

Including a pilot period in the program provides a way to address resistances and develop a secure understanding of potential problems. No decisions are irrevocable. Faculty members may be willing to forestall objections if they are assured that an evaluation of the proposed program will provide data to enable them to judge the program's merits and anticipate problems in course implementation.

At one institution in the Cultural Legacies project, several departments that had courses or topical areas overlapping with the interdisciplinary courses proposed for the new core refused at first to submit new courses, preferring to lobby for keeping their own courses as an elective to fulfill general-education requirements. After the pilot period, however, the new program proved very successful with students and faculty members, and some faculty members from resistant departments began to submit courses to count under the new core program.

It is during the pilot phase that logistical issues become clear. Core requirements for students who transfer to the institution is a good example. Well-integrated and comprehensive core programs that extend beyond the first year of a student's program pose particularly difficult problems for transfer students, since the sophomore- and junior-year experiences draw on knowledge and skills taught in earlier parts of the sequence. During the pilot phase, a subcommittee of the core committee should investigate the profiles of transfer students and develop a proposal for options they can use to fulfill core requirements.

Logistical issues are legitimate concerns, but they should not be allowed to defeat the proposal. Core committees will have to be prepared to address them during the presentation of the proposal to the faculty. SUNY–Buffalo and Tufts University were particularly creative in publishing and circulating lists of commonly asked questions about the core along with responses from the committee. At Tufts, for example, some of the questions included: Why does a decision have to be made at this time?

Does implementation of a requirement in World Civilizations add to the number of required courses a student will have to take? Will this impose a requirement in which students have no choice? Has the Western tradition been excluded or slighted in World Civilizations courses? How large will classes be? Who will be teaching World Civilization classes? How will staffing of the World Civilization courses affect the departments? Can Tufts afford this program?

Experimentation with different teaching styles (team-teaching or combinations of large lecture and small discussion sections, for example) during the pilot phase allows planners to refine pedagogical techniques and provides data to convince faculty members of the soundness of choices in light of the philosophical underpinnings of the program and the resources available to support it. A pilot period also allows for astute faculty development linked to the goals, course content, and pedagogical strategies of the program.

STAFFING THE NEW CORE PROGRAMS

Given the multiple goals of integrated core courses, faculty members working on core design and implementation argue strongly for the importance of small sections of fifteen to twenty-five students for at least a part of the program. Many institutions are successfully combining large lecture sections for all students in the course with small discussion sections once or twice per week. It is necessary, therefore, to develop a cadre of people with responsibility for the program and ensure an adequate number of trained faculty members to teach in the core program.

In some cases, graduate teaching assistants staff courses or sections. At the University of Kansas, for example, graduate teaching assistants staff all the sections of the Western Civilization course except the honors section. At Washington State University, English graduate assistants have full responsibility for the composition course "Writing about the World," which also develops critical thinking skills through class discussion; they receive extensive training the summer before they teach to prepare them for their role. Graduate assistants serve as section leaders at Tufts University and SUNY–Buffalo. At smaller institutions such as the University of North Carolina–Asheville, Fairleigh Dickinson University, and the University of Richmond, humanities faculty members lead the sections themselves.

Since it is likely that fiscal restraints will hamper curriculum planning well into the future, institutions would do well to experiment with innovative ways of staffing sections of courses or breaking larger sections into groups during class periods. Using advanced undergraduate students as well as graduate students as teachers and discussion leaders is one possibility. There are many educational as well as fiscal benefits to this approach. Students learn more when they prepare to present material than simply by studying it; they also are more likely to ask questions and venture hypotheses with peers than with faculty members. Students may be motivated to expend more effort if they know that their work is going to be scrutinized by peers and may learn more course material in greater depth if they help teach it to fellow students.

Strong programs of faculty and teaching-assistant development are essential to effective teaching in core programs. Faculty development ensures an adequate pool of teachers for core programs and continuity during sabbaticals, leaves, and turnover. It also acquaints faculty members with teaching techniques that employ collaborative learning and peer teaching.

If these new core programs live up to their promise of becoming the intellectual center of the campus, involving students in effective communities, and preparing them for civic responsibilities, they might well replace some of the activities currently sponsored by the student services division by default. It may be possible, then, to reduce the amount of programming in student services and reallocate funds to core programs and general-education curricula—or to jointly sponsor such programs.

BUILDING ASSESSMENT INTO THE PLAN

Building formal evaluation activities into the design and implementation of core courses is an essential means of gauging progress, guiding decisions for future activities, and providing information to both supporters and critics of the program about its strengths and weaknesses. In many cases, assessment in the Cultural Legacies project, like the new pedagogies, became collaborative.

At Mount St. Mary's College (Md.), for example, faculty members teaching in the core work together as a group to judge its effectiveness. At the beginning of the term, faculty members review the goals for each course and the means for attaining them. During regular staff meetings, these faculty members discuss the texts being used, student reactions, what difficulties exist, what works and what does not work. At the end of each term, the coordinator of each course prepares a formal report that reflects the judgment of the faculty members about the overall success of the course. Recommendations for change emanate from this ongoing process of review, as well as from traditional student evaluations of professors and core courses.

The Carthage College Heritage Studies program developed a new questionnaire to assess student understanding of the goals and methods of the courses and student perceptions of the effectiveness of the learning environment created in the Heritage Studies seminars. Questions included:

- How would you explain the goals, methods, and expectations of Heritage I to a prospective new student?

- Which course materials—*Heart of Darkness*, *Things Fall Apart*, *Apocalypse Now*, films, videos, works of art, musical selections—did you find most appropriate for learning about culture and communication? Why? Which did you find least appropriate? Why?

- What do you think is the most important insight that you've gained about the way you write through Heritage Studies so far?

- What do you think is the most important insight that you've gained through Heritage Studies about the ways you communicate orally? about listening?

- Do you think your teacher tried to create a learning environment in which you felt encouraged and challenged to work together in groups with other students, both in and out of class?

- Do you think your teacher respected the idea that each student has unique talents and unique ways of learning?

- Do you think your teacher tried to create a learning environment within which students showed respect for each other's differences in culture, race, gender, values?

- Do you think your teacher tried to create a learning environment within which you could question and even challenge the ideas of others, including the teacher, other students, authors of class materials?

- Did you feel free to speak up and ask questions if you didn't understand something?

For those institutions implementing new programs, especially when the pilot phase is a test of the effectiveness of a particular model, data on specific student outcomes might be desirable. George Mason University designed an extensive assessment of its linked courses, Core 100 (composition) and Core 103 ("Presence of the Past"), that included these components:

- focus groups with both students and faculties of each of the pilot courses to monitor progress toward course goals

- focus groups with faculty members led by an external evaluator

- surveys of student reasons for enrollment
- pre- and post-course writing attitude survey
- evaluation of student writing portfolios (Core 100)
- assessment of a random sample of final papers (Core 103)
- a survey of student satisfaction with the course at the end of the term.

Interactive assessment methods that involve discussions among faculty members and between students and faculty members become opportunities for learning, as well as for making improvements in the courses. The benefit of this kind of assessment is that it generates a *collective* responsibility for the quality and effectiveness of student learning.

Some of the institutions in the Cultural Legacies project conducted research studies to determine specific student learning outcomes of the core program. At Fairleigh Dickinson University, for example, researchers studied the influence of African American authors on students in the core curriculum. By comparing pre- and post-program essays about influential ideas, the researchers concluded that reading literature by African American authors in a core curriculum has potential for changing student attitudes and behaviors.[40]

Most institutions in the project found it helpful to invite outside consultants—individuals with extensive experience in core programs—to review the program and make suggestions for change. These consultants conducted focus groups, sat in on classes, interviewed faculty members and students, met with administrators, and reviewed program reports and self-studies in an attempt to gain a comprehensive view of how well the program was functioning and what kinds of changes would improve it. External evaluators' views usually carried more weight with faculty decision-making groups because of the impartial, comparative perspectives they brought to bear on the analysis of program strengths and weaknesses.

ALLOCATING RESOURCES

Most of the institutions in the Cultural Legacies project, like colleges and universities all over the country, are experiencing very difficult times financially. One institution did not progress very far in its design because of the degree to which the nationwide recession affected state budgets for education. This state university lost faculty positions and, as a result, was forced to increase faculty teaching loads. In addition, there were no funds from faculty development to allow rethinking curricular design and instructional approaches. Still, the team leader was able to cite progress in curriculum development through participation in the AAC project, assistance from the institution's consultant, and models from other campuses. His main task for the future, as he sees it, is to support the pockets of energy that still exist and the faculty members who are making changes. Small grants from a number of sources are helping.

Design phase. The degree to which a core design committee considers resource restraints depends on the charge it is given by the administration. A good administrator will ask the committee to begin by thinking about the best program for the students at that point in time, without being overly constrained by financial concerns. When departments are taking significant cuts from their budgets, reducing programs and faculty, and operating on a shoestring, however, it may be hard for core planners to take this advice. Yet a faculty committee that begins with the question of what is *realistic* probably will not get beyond tinkering with current courses and credits, patching together a core program that is less than what the institution can implement and certainly less than what students need and faculty members want. One of the greatest temptations for program planners is using existing courses to fulfill new course requirements and limiting the reform to developing a new set of criteria for faculty members to use in revising pre-existing, departmentally-based courses for the new program.

Even in times of adequate resources, it is important to begin with fundamental questions about institutional mission, goals for student learning, and curricular and pedagogical strengths of the faculty. Allowing curriculum planners to focus on what is intellectually compelling and educationally sound rather than on the numbers of faculty members and sections needed to staff a specific course is a better assurance that a good program will result from their deliberations. Their task at the outset is to use their imagination to create and innovate; it is then the task of the implementation committee and administrators to translate the dream into decisions about resource allocation.

Once the program has begun to take shape—and before faculty members invest too much time deciding on the logistics of staffing—the appropriate administrative staff or committee should begin to estimate costs. Richard Kamber, dean of arts and sciences at Trenton State College, points out that knowledge about the actual costs of the program is important—not just because it warns planners away from a scale of activity that may not be advisable or feasible but also because this knowledge is "powerful in terms of planning, powerful in terms of influencing the future course of the institution, and powerful in helping you to make business-like decisions about what you can keep and what you can afford to give up."[41]

The numbers help stifle the complaints that plague any new initiative from those who have not bought into the process: "It's too expensive," "It's a good idea, but we can't afford it." In making decisions to vote for a program or for a pilot of a program, faculty governance bodies will certainly ask what the new program will cost in relation to the curriculum that is in place. What are the *additional* costs, and where will the resources to pay for them come from?

Every institution has particularities in the way that it budgets and tracks curriculum costs, and every institution with good budgeting and accounting processes and procedures is able to answer questions about costs, and cost-effectiveness, of new programs. Each methodology will be institution-specific but will involve making assumptions about projected student enrollments in the institution during the pilot and implementation phases of the new program, costs of each faculty teaching slot in the old program and in the new program, and enrollments in the new program. This last item is more predictable when new courses are required than when they are in a pilot stage; the more choices allowed for students in core programs, the more difficulty there will be in estimating the numbers of students to expect in core courses.

Once the figures are determined, they can guide decisions about the number of students in each section, program staffing (for example, having all classes in small sections or using a combination of large lectures and small discussion sessions), the feasibility of team-teaching, the use of part-time faculty members and teaching assistants, and so forth. This is the phase in which the give-and-take of ideal program versus real program begins. Compromises in pedagogical principles may be made in order to afford the start-up of a program, keeping in mind that the ideal might be phased in when resources are available. For example, faculty members may compromise on course enrollment caps of twenty-five students, when eighteen to twenty would be ideal for the course methods.

Resources for program start-up and maintenance—beyond staffing costs—must be taken into account. To ensure faculty commitment to program development and implementation, administrators must commit adequate resources at the beginning of the process and ensure that funds will be available to sustain the program. Programs need resources for:

- released time and/or stipends for faculty members to develop new subject matter expertise

- released time for faculty members teaching new courses
- outside speakers and consultants for faculty seminars
- texts and other preparatory materials for faculty members teaching new courses
- library acquisitions to support student and faculty research in new areas
- released time and summer salary for a faculty coordinator of the program, or salary for an administrative line
- secretarial support
- an operations budget for course materials and dissemination such as a core newsletter or flyers to advertise core events
- travel funds for faculty members to attend professional meetings related to core curriculum development; visits to peer institutions.

The costs of development and training in the pilot years can amount to between $25,000 and $75,000 per year, depending on the cost of the coordinator position and the number of faculty members receiving stipends or released time for course development and piloting.

Implementation. Ultimately, resources will have to be redirected from existing sources, most of which are in departmental budgets. In most of the successful programs in the Cultural Legacies project, administrators with control over institutional funds worked to strengthen academic departments at the same time they built a strong core program. These administrators worked with department chairs or heads to find ways to achieve departmental curricular goals while finding ways for the department to contribute to the core. Incentives such as teaching assistant lines, full replacement costs for faculty members teaching in the core, or new lines to hire faculty members with expertise in core areas as well as in areas the department wishes to develop are very attractive to departments. At one campus, a core program gave one course hour of released time for each semester a faculty member taught in the core. After three years, core teachers had earned a semester off from teaching to pursue their research.

The ultimate challenge for the institution is to connect the entire curriculum in a meaningful way, so that general education is not viewed as subordinate to the major but as equally fundamental to the undergraduate degree. Resource allocation for core studies and general education will be less contested if the curriculum is seen as a whole with complementary and intertwining parts, rather than as two separate and competing domains.

SUSTAINING THE PROGRAM

Just as implementation considerations must be built into the design phase, implementation decisions must be made with a view toward sustaining the program over time. A plan for permanent support of the program must emerge during the pilot period. Putting in place an ambitious program that relies heavily on outside grant funds but is too expensive for the institution to sustain in its pilot configuration is self-defeating. Core planners need to address essential supports that ensure both the quality and the viability of the program: policy, personnel, resources, governance structure, program review, and faculty/student involvement. Here are some examples of the kinds of support needed for sustaining strong core programs:

Policy

- Require training of new faculty members who teach in core courses.

- Make considerations of candidates' expertise in core areas part of the interview process for all new faculty members.

- Charge a faculty committee with responsibility to review, assess, and improve the program.

- Incorporate criteria related to successful teaching in core programs as part of tenure and promotion guidelines and regular merit review.

- Establish a decision-making structure for making changes in the core.

Personnel

- Provide at least a half-time director or coordinator of the core program, with appropriate compensation in the form of salary and/or released time.

- Assign adequate staff support for the core: secretarial support, research support, materials development support, and faculty development support.

- Include core areas of expertise in long-term planning about allocation of positions.

Resources

- Assign a separate budget to support the core under the appropriate administrator.

- Provide funds for adequate staff and teaching personnel, faculty development, travel, course activities (field trips, films), and operations.

Governance structure

- Create a representative advisory or oversight committee (whichever fits with the culture of the institution and the structure of the core).

- Clearly delineate the responsibilities of the committee and its reporting relationship to administrators or to established curriculum committees or other standing faculty committees.

- Appoint students to the committees, or create a student advisory committee.

Program review

- Establish mechanisms for reviewing the success of the program.

- Establish clear goals for assessment (student satisfaction, student outcomes, faculty satisfaction, faculty quality, and so forth) and design a process that yields appropriate information.

- Include reviews that are both internal and external to the program and to the institution. Use recognized experts with good knowledge of practice nationally.

- Include a review of the core program in institutional self-studies and accreditation reviews. These reviews should always have program improvement as the primary goal.

- Involve as many faculty members as possible in learning from the results.

Faculty/student involvement

- Design activities that make the core a central part of the intellectual life of the campus, such as distinguished lecture series, faculty/student research conferences, a core program on the campus radio station, or social gatherings for faculty members and students.

- Continue to involve faculty members and students in ongoing evaluation of the program to sustain ownership.

- Participate as an institution in national networks and programs—such as the Cultural Legacies project—to keep abreast of good practice in undergraduate education.

To maintain programs of common learning, faculty leaders must pay constant attention to communicating the aims of the program with the various constituencies in the institution. Merritt Moseley, former director of the Humanities Program at the University of North Carolina–Asheville, summarizes the necessary elements: "The governing assumptions must be made clear; they must be widely shared. Making sure that all faculty understand them is a good idea, both for their own peace of mind and because of their importance in helping *students* to understand what they are engaged in and how it connects to the mission of the university."

Moseley also argues for the necessity of making the director or coordinator of the core program an active participant in hiring decisions and in deans' and chairs' meetings. If core programs are to sustain their visibility and become central to the intellectual vitality of the campus, strong leadership is important. There should be one person with administrative responsibility for the program who serves as its advocate within the administration and involves faculty members who govern the program in decision making.

FUTURE CORE PROGRAM STRUCTURES

One of the implementation issues this guide has skirted is clearly defining the direction in which core programs are heading in terms of an effective administrative structure. For the most part, colleges and universities in the United States still are heavily controlled by departments, and general education and core programs still are seen as subordinate to the major. Readers of earlier drafts of this manuscript rightly pointed out that this traditional structure is effectively reinforced by recommending that departments be given incentives to "release" faculty members for the core and faculty members who teach in the core be rewarded with research leave. While core planners in the Cultural Legacies project saw no other means of operating within current structures, many were adamant that these departmentally based structures, and the ways they partition knowledge, were not adequate to the kind of teaching necessary in interdisciplinary core programs engaging cultural multiplicity.

Bari Watkins, vice president for academic affairs at Queens College (N.C.), proposes an interim solution: the hiring of faculty members into interdisciplinary core programs. Queens College has made one such hire. Watkins notes that this process could help institutions find better candidates for a deliberately interdisciplinary program; more importantly, she suggests that "searches for these positions would help all of us send a message to the graduate programs that faculty with interdisciplinary interests and concern for liberal arts teaching are not at an automatic disadvantage in the job market."

A more modest approach, which Queens College also employs, is to include a statement in all advertisements for faculty positions that the college is seeking candidates who are interested in teaching in the core program at some time during their academic career. For liberal arts institutions, this kind of announcement draws candidates with broadly based academic interests and screens out individuals who wish to focus their teaching and research in highly specialized areas. Large universities will have to experiment with diversification of faculty contracts and job descriptions to accomplish the multiple goals of excellence in teaching, research, and service.

The structure of core programs within the institution and the rewards for faculty members who contribute to them must be a central agenda for national discussion and action among higher education leaders. Core studies and/or general education represent between 30 and 60 percent of a typical undergraduate student's education. Until colleges and universities ensure that this portion of the curriculum is of high quality and well integrated into students' total educational experience, students will continue to view these courses as subjects to be gotten out of the way before embarking on their "real" programs, and institutions will miss a central opportunity to communicate to students what is of value for citizens who wish to lead full lives and contribute to their communities in an increasingly complex and interdependent world.

TIPS FOR PROGRAM IMPLEMENTATION: DO'S AND DON'TS

There is no one "best" strategy or mix of strategies that will ensure successful implementation of a core curriculum that engages cultural pluralism. In spite of strong leadership, careful planning, collaborative processes, and adequate resources, the core curriculum may not pass, or it may not be fully implemented. Potential pitfalls include shifts in political power within the institution, reorganization of administrative units, loss of resources due to shortfalls or cutbacks, changes in the administration, or well-mounted attacks from opposing groups that result in loss of administrative or faculty support. Success has a lot to do with good timing and with careful maneuvering when the unpredictable surfaces. Still, there are some tips that core planners can follow to enhance the likelihood of passing and implementing a new core program.

Don't

- avoid essential intellectual and political issues
- design program goals that are too ambitious for the institution, the faculty, and the students
- assume support on the part of any constituency (*do* check it out!)
- rely on token rather than real administrative support
- rely on any one constituency
- convey mixed messages about the importance of the core or of engaging cultural multiplicity in the core
- try to do to much too soon with too few resources
- proceed in a financial and institutional vacuum

Do

- develop a collaborative planning process that includes analysis, design, pilot, and implementation phases
- develop consensus about the need for change
- clearly define the scope of the proposed core and how it will benefit students
- include all constituencies in the needs assessment process
- build ownership among the faculty through consultation at key points in the process
- set up clear channels of communication between the faculty and the administration
- secure adequate resources for all phases of the planning and implementation process
- set realistic time lines
- delineate lines of authority and accountability for the process
- build in key decisions points and collect the necessary data to allow decision makers to act
- respect the integrity of institutional processes and procedures
- communicate regularly with all interested groups and take advantage of opportunities to publicize program successes.

5 Features of Strong Programs

A review of curriculum planning and implementation at the institutions participating in the Cultural Legacies project suggests that strong core programs are never "finished." They are vital, alive, and ever-changing as a result of constant review and improvement. Periodically, substantial revisions or new models may be implemented. Stability comes from the expertise and commitment of the faculty, not from the content of a syllabus.

Experimentation with new frameworks for engaging cultural pluralism will continue to challenge curriculum planners well into the future. Nonetheless, even within a context of educational evolution and change, strong core programs typically exhibit certain features.

- Strong core programs define a set of courses that reflect faculty consensus about areas of knowledge essential for a liberal education, including attention to the study of world cultures and U.S. pluralism. These programs use a relational approach rather than an additive approach to the study of cultural experience and human difference and engage commonality in and through difference rather than promulgating a unitary model that denies the multiplicity of cultures.

- In forging new content paradigms, strong core programs delineate with clarity how the core curriculum embodies the educational philosophy, mission, and historic identity of the institution.

- Strong programs base their structure and content on an analysis and understanding of student needs and characteristics, as well as upon their institutional philosophy of education. Periodic assessments of student profiles, with specific attention to the diversity of student characteristics and backgrounds, contribute to discussions of curricular revision.

- Strong core programs deliberately draw upon successful curricular initiatives and faculty expertise in areas such as writing, ethnic studies, women's studies, international studies, and collaborative learning.

- Strong core programs have effective leaders. Program leaders have positions of influence on campus, serve as advocates for the program, seek input from all sectors, and maintain effective and productive relationships with academic administrators.

- Strong core programs define the kinds and levels of skills students are expected to acquire in specific courses and design pedagogies to accomplish skill-related goals. Faculty members rethink skill development within the context of multiculturalism. There is systematic and comprehensive attention to oral and written communication skills. Many programs include development of research and library skills as central elements in the core program.

- Strong core programs engage students in the study and analysis of primary texts—fiction, poetry, historical documents, works of art— drawn from many cultures and many disciplines.

- Strong core programs include enough courses and credit hours to accomplish the goals of the program and avoid overburdening a small set of courses or including goals that sound good on paper but are unattainable in reality.

- Strong core programs sequence courses vertically over three or four years of the undergraduate experience. Many are adopting an interdisciplinary capstone course, either within the core or within the academic major, that explores contemporary issues or problems and draws upon both the content and the skills students have learned throughout their programs of study.

- Strong core programs connect learning across disciplines and develop structures that enable faculty members and students to make connections between and among areas of knowledge. Interdisciplinary, thematic, and clustered- or linked-course approaches are common means to achieve the integration of knowledge in the core.

- Strong core programs are linked with academic majors as essential and complementary parts of undergraduate education. The institution treats these two areas as mutually reinforcing. Core program directors work with academic administrators to ensure that issues of departmental curricula and faculty workload are successfully resolved and that contributions to the core have benefits for the traditional departments.

- Strong core programs use a range of pedagogies, including cooperative and collaborative learning activities. Faculty members in these programs use collaborative learning activities to build intellectual and social community and responsibility among students.

- Strong core programs contribute to the development and support of an intellectual community on campus by establishing a framework for common learning, structures that encourage faculty and student interaction across departments and fields, and public events that draw all members of the community together.

- Strong core programs have sufficient and predictable resources. Resource allocation is tied into the institutional review and planning process.

- Strong core programs invest in faculty development programs to assist intructors in learning new content areas and new collaborative learning techniques.

- Strong core programs conduct periodic assessments that include information on program strengths and weaknesses from students and faculty members.

SHORT-TERM INDICATORS OF SUCCESS

While many of the core programs in the Cultural Legacies project illustrate these features or are well on their way toward these goals, not all of the participating institutions are as far along. On many campuses, the design for the core, while incorporating these features, is still on the drawing board. On others, core courses are being piloted, but their eventual adoption as part of a core program or general education is not assured. Most of the core programs that are in place—at both resource and planning institutions in the project—are still being regularly reviewed and revised.

While keeping a long-term vision as a guidepost, it is important for core program planners to pay attention to the short-term benefits of core

review processes and course development. There are many positive benefits that occur during the design, piloting, and implementation process that
should not be discounted, even if a program does not pass a faculty vote or
stalls in its implementation for other reasons. It is important for institutional and faculty morale to recognize what has been done along the way.
As one dean notes, "If we never fully implement this program, it will have
been worth it just in terms of the intellectual stimulation of faculty."

Here are short-term indicators of success that can serve to reward
those involved in the process:

- A decision on the part of the faculty and the administration to
  implement a program of common learning for at least a portion of
  the undergraduate general-education curriculum

- Active involvement of a significant number of faculty members

- The building of an effective faculty-administrative alliance

- Faculty development in areas of cultural pluralism and teaching in
  multicultural settings

- Consensus about institutional mission, student learning goals, and
  discussions about students and their needs

- Modifications made to the existing curriculum that reflect features
  of strong core programs

- Putting in place administrative structures to ensure ongoing
  change

- Securing administrative commitment and resources for future
  change.

If an institution does not have a climate to support major curricular change, investing in faculty development that leads to individual
improvements in courses of programs—both in content and pedagogy—is
an essential means of building strength that will serve programs well in
the future.

Afterword: Challenges for the Future

by Carol G. Schneider and Betty Schmitz

AAC's Cultural Legacies project provides a glimpse of core curriculum reform at a moment of dramatic transition in higher education in the United States. Colleges and universities in the project are addressing both fragmentation and ethnocentrism in undergraduate education by developing interdisciplinary core courses that engage cultural multiplicity and interconnections. In so doing, they are attempting to come to terms with the intellectual and curricular implications of a new social and political consciousness of cultural pluralism at home and abroad. In these programs, a dialogic model for engaging culture is fast replacing a unitary model.

The excitement of engaging cultural pluralism in the content and structures of core curricula has led not to a new paradigm for their central focus but to great intellectual vitality. The reach of new core programs extends well beyond the current expertise of faculties; part of the excitement comes from the fact that faculty members themselves are enlarging their own academic interests and expertise along both cultural and interdisciplinary lines. Forward-thinking institutions are developing programs that build upon the energies and expertise of their current faculty members while asking themselves what the composition and expertise of the faculty should be in the early decades of the twenty-first century. The answer to this question guides faculty development and hiring as well as resource allocation.

As we have seen in our review of institutions participating in the Cultural Legacies project, there has been more extensive work on reconceiving Western and world cultures than on U.S. pluralism. Only a quarter of the institutions in the project developed courses that primarily address the historical roots and contemporary contexts of U.S. pluralism. This relative imbalance reflects a historical trend in general-education programs. In part because secondary schools are far more likely to teach U.S. history than European or world history, college-level general-education courses typically have sought to redress the balance.

Civilization courses in college have routinely taught Europe, less often the United States.

This inherited inclination to focus on cultures outside the United States serves the nation poorly in an era of rapidly changing consciousness about the multiple social, cultural, and political dimensions of our own diversity. Even at institutions addressing the U.S. in new core courses, there is a remarkable absence of attention to the meanings and responsibilities of citizenship in a multicultural society. In the syllabi reviewed for this study, civic values, virtues, and institutions frequently seem to be an assumed background rather than an essential foreground for explorations of diversity. Too often, democracy and democratic pluralism are taken as givens—not as hard-won, historically situated values and practices still in negotiation in this country and internationally. Reading a handful of great texts in U.S. history, as a few programs require, will not provide students with either the knowledge or the competencies that participation in a pluralistic democracy requires.

Current social and political events dramatically illustrate that we must redefine what core values our cultural systems embed. Democracy, as we know, does not function optimally for all our citizens. Members of different cultural groups, differentially situated relative to power and status, have very different beliefs about the causes, manifestations, extent, and remedies for social, political, and economic inequities. Yet few of us have had formal multicultural educational experiences that enable us to deal with these realities of cultural, political, and economic diversity as they affect our moral and civic responsibilities.

Core programs ought to give sustained attention to the connections between cultural knowledge and civic competencies and responsibilities. As we saw in Chapter 2, Michael Morris has argued that citizens in our society need new understandings and competencies—including interdependence, collaboration, holistic vision, cross-cultural and intercultural communication, consensus decision making, and community-global thinking. While others might construct this list differently, each core program should have its own understanding of the knowledge and capabilities basic to our diverse society. Each program should be able to explain what practices and assignments in the program foster these capabilities in students.

Core curricula also must devote new attention to communities, especially communities within the United States. As we have seen, there is an increasing emphasis on building learning communities in the new core programs. This emphasis, however—focusing on classroom dynamics and collaborative learning—largely ignores the multicultural nature of students' values and backgrounds. Very few programs address students' experiences as participants in multiple communities: different, overlapping, sometimes competing or estranged. Programs designed to address multiplicity and diversity must take the pluralism of United States communities seriously as experiential realities for students.

Negotiating one's affinities and commitments to diverse communities within U.S. society is a challenge for all citizens—and a special challenge for liberal education. Crossing borders and boundaries, working cross-culturally, negotiating difference, sustaining multiple and perhaps competing commitments, developing one's value system while honoring that of others, making consequential choices while recognizing significant disagreement, sustaining a sense of relation to the entire polity: These are some of the societal requirements confronting curricula engaging cultural pluralism in the U.S.

There are many questions about U.S. pluralism that are yet to be fully answered by the majority of institutions in this country.

- What kinds of content and organization of content help students grasp the historical and contemporary contexts of cultural pluralism in the United States?

- What do students need to know about the historical roots and contemporary contexts of social, political, and economic inequities in the United States?

- What do students need to know about the historical and contemporary constructs of ethnicity, gender, race, class, sexual orientation, and other variables of human identity?

- What do students need to know about the major American racial and ethnic groups and intra-ethnic variations?

- What kinds of competencies will graduates need to negotiate their disparate and multiple commitments and communities, inherited or adopted?

- What kinds of intercultural competencies are required for full participation in a pluralist society? What kinds of values?

- What kinds of intercultural competencies are required to work within diverse organizations? How can core programs help students acquire these competencies?

- What kinds of pedagogy are effective in multicultural classrooms? For teaching cultural pluralism? For teaching new civic competencies?

- What is the difference between recognizing and acknowledging difference and learning to take grounded stances in the face of difference? If both are goals for liberal learning, how are we going to help students develop these capabilities over time?

- What is the academy's responsibility to advance values that foster democratic and cultural pluralism? Faculty members' responsibilities? How and where are these matters addressed by faculties and academic administrators? How are they addressed within the larger society?

We stand at the beginning of a process of rethinking core curricula nationally. Such rethinking inevitably both reflects and imparts a sense of the important questions confronting our society. Liberal learning, as it manifests itself in approaches to general education, has always championed intellectual diversity as indispensible in fostering critical thinking and grounded analysis. Faculty members across the country are expanding their horizons to address and incorporate the diversity of cultural heritages in the United States and around the world. Our challenge for the future is to connect this new attention to cultural pluralism with our long-standing U.S. commitment to democratic pluralism. We must seek—not just as colleges but as a society—the intellectual, interpersonal, and civic learning that can sustain and renew a multicultural democracy.

Appendix:
Project Participants

RESOURCE INSTITUTIONS AND CONSULTANTS

City University of New York–Queens College
Anne Dobbs (Romance Languages); *Elaine Maimon* (English),
Dean of Experimental Programs; *Anthony O'Brien* (English)

Columbia University
Jacob Smit (History), Director of the Core Program;
Kathryn Yatrakis, Associate Dean of the Curriculum

Earlham College
Peter Cline (History);
Robert Johnstone (Politics); *Daniel Meerson* (English)

Fairleigh Dickinson University*
John Becker (Philosophy), Director, University Core Program;
Leonard Grob (Philosophy), Director, University Core Program;
Geoffrey Weinman, Vice President for Academic Affairs

Mount St. Mary's College (Md.)
William J. Craft (English); *Thomas F. Flynn*, Dean of the College

Queens College (N.C.)
Charles Reed (History), Director, Liberal Learning Program;
Bari Watkins, Vice President for Academic Affairs;
Robert Whalen (History)

State University of New York–Buffalo*
Jeannette Ludwig (Modern Languages & Literature), Associate
Vice Provost; *John Meacham* (Psychology)

University of Denver
James Kirk (Religious Studies); *Jere Surber* (Philosophy)

University of Kansas
Robert Anderson (French and Italian Studies); *James Woelfel*
(Philosophy), Director of the Western Civilization Program

University of North Carolina–Asheville
Margaret J. Downes (Literature); *Merritt Moseley* (Literature)

---

*These universities were planning institutions in the first round of the project; they served
as resource institutions in the second round.

Washington State University
Richard Haswell (History); *Richard Law*, Director of General
Education, Division of Humanities and Social Sciences;
Alice Spitzer, Reference Librarian

PLANNING INSTITUTIONS (ROUND ONE)

Beaver College

Brandeis University

Carnegie Mellon University

Carthage College

College of St. Catherine

College of St. Francis

Drake University

Fairleigh Dickinson University*

George Mason University

Hampton University

LeMoyne-Owen College

Lesley College

Massachusetts Bay Community College

Oglethorpe University

Otterbein College

Samford University

Spelman College

St. Lawrence University

State University of New York–Buffalo*

Tennessee State University

University of Alaska–Fairbanks

University of Oklahoma

University of Richmond

University of Wyoming

Utah State University

Wesleyan College

Western Washington University

PLANNING INSTITUTIONS (ROUND TWO)

Adelphi University

Atlanta College of Art

Auburn University

Birmingham-Southern College

City University of New York–Brooklyn College

Ferrum College

Franklin Pierce College

Goshen College

Goucher College

Hood College

Kent State University, Regional Campuses

Long Island University, Brooklyn Campus

Louisiana State University

Mount Vernon College

North Dakota State University

Northeastern University

Saint Edward's University

State University of New York–College at New Paltz

State University of New York–College at Oswego

Trenton State College

Tufts University

University of California–Los Angeles

University of Evansville

University of Montana

University of Texas–El Paso

Ursuline College

Whitman College

Notes

1. Association of American Colleges, internal report, 11 July 1990.
2. See the section on undergraduate curriculum in the selected bibliography (pages 121–122).
3. Task Group on General Education, *A New Vitality in General Education* (Washington: Association of American Colleges, 1988), 1.
4. "Discussing Diversity," *Liberal Education* 77 (January/February 1991): 2.
5. Carnegie Foundation for the Advancement of Teaching, "Signs of a Changing Curriculum," *Change* 24 (January/February 1992): 49–52.
6. Arthur Levine and Jeannette Cureton, "The Quiet Revolution: Eleven Facts About Multiculturalism and the Curriculum," *Change* 24 (January/February 1992): 24–30.
7. Jerry G. Gaff, "Beyond Politics: The Educational Issues Inherent in Multicultural Education," *Change* 24 (January/February 1992): 31.
8. See Betty Schmitz, *Integrating Women's Studies into the Curriculum: A Guide and Bibliography* (Old Westbury, N.Y.: Feminist Press, 1985); Johnnella E. Butler and John C. Walter, *Transforming the Curriculum: Ethnic Studies and Women's Studies* (Albany, N.Y.: State University of New York Press, 1991).
9. Personal communication, 20 September 1991.
10. This textbook, edited by James Woelfel (current director of the Western Civilization Program) and Sarah Chappell Trulove, was published by Ginn Press in 1991. Faculty members planning interdisciplinary core programs have reported difficulties in locating appropriate texts or collections of readings. There are several narrative textbooks suitable for Western civilization courses, but most are humanities focused rather than interdisciplinary, and they often are less multicultural than faculty members would like. On some campuses, faculty members have added inexpensive paperback editions of individual texts; achieving the necessary variety of texts, however, can make these courses too costly for students.

   Many core programs have created their own readers, finding mainstream publishers to produce them or securing permission to reproduce materials locally. Increasingly, faculty members want to produce locally photocopied packets or collections of primary and secondary texts. The National Association of College Stores, Association of American Publishers, and Association of American University Presses have published a guide to reproducing copyrighted materials, *Questions and Answers on Copyright for the Campus Community* (available from NACS, 500 East Lorain Street, Oberlin, OH 44074-1294). There also are presses that specialize in producing legal, customized texts for campuses; for example, Tapestry Press (P.O. Box 1113, Acton, MA 01720; telephone 1-800-535-2007) will handle copyright matters and produce customized textbooks.
11. Western Washington University, internal memo shared with AAC.
12. "Recentering Within the Western Tradition" (Presentation at the 77th Annual Meeting of the Association of American Colleges, Washington, D.C., 13 January 1991).
13. Letter to Karen Klein, Brandeis University, 21 January 1992.
14. Organization of American Historians, *Restoring Women to History: Teaching Packets for Integrating Women's History into Courses on Africa, Asia, Latin America, the Caribbean, and the Middle East* (Bloomington, Ind.: OAH, 1988). See also Elizabeth Fox-Genovese and Susan Mosher Stuard, *Restoring Women to History: Materials for Western Civilization I and II*, 2 vols. (Bloomington, Ind.: OAH 1983).
15. The Southwest Institute for Research on Women at the University of Arizona, for example, has conducted several curriculum transformation projects, including ones to integrate gender into international and world studies.
16. "The Difficult Dialogue of Curriculum Transformation," in *Transforming the Curriculum: Ethnic Studies and Women's Studies*, ed. Johnnella E. Butler and John C. Walter (Albany, N.Y.: State University of New York Press, 1991), 5.
17. Nancy B. Black and Michael R. Mills, "Inspiring Teachers to Revitalize Teaching," in *Liberating Education*, Zelda Gamson, et al. (San Francisco: Jossey-Bass, 1984), 112.
18. Alexander Astin, *What Matters in College: Four Critical Years Revisited* (San Francisco: Jossey-Bass, 1992); Ernest T. Pascarella and Patrick T. Terenzini, *How College Affects Students* (San Francisco: Jossey-Bass, 1991).
19. Zelda Gamson, *Liberating Education* (San Francisco: Jossey-Bass, 1984), xv.

20. Jerry Gaff and Thomas Klein, *Reforming General Education: A Survey* (San Francisco: Jossey-Bass, 1982).

21. For a survey and review of collaborative learning in its different forms and structures, see Barbara Leigh Smith and Jean T. MacGregor, "What is Collaborative Learning?" in *Collaborative Learning: A Sourcebook for Higher Education*, ed. Anne Goodsell, Michelle Maher, and Vincent Tinto (Syracuse, N.Y.: National Center on Postsecondary Teaching, Learning and Assessment, 1992).

22. Internal document shared with AAC, "Planning Our Future" (Fall 1989), 8–9.

23. Patrick J. Hill, "Multiculturalism: The Crucial Philosophical and Organizational Issues," *Change* 23 (July/August 1991): 39–47.

24. *A New Vitality*, 11.

25. This textbook, edited by Susan McLeod with four teaching assistants, was published by Harcourt, Brace, Jovanovich in 1991.

26. Minnich, "Discussing Diversity," 5.

27. "A Work in Progress: The New Civic Competencies" (Paper presented to the National Society for Internships and Experiential Education, Santa Fe, N.M., 27 October 1989).

28. Quoted from the program brochure.

29. Smith and MacGregor, "What is Collaborative Learning?"

30. "On the Genealogy of Teaching" (article published in the University of Richmond's *Arts and Sciences* newsletter).

31. Karen T. Romer, "Collaboration: New Forms of Learning, New Ways of Thinking," *Forum for Liberal Education* 8 (November/December 1985): 3. This issue of *Forum* includes a list of resources.

32. Zelda F. Gamson and Patrick J. Hill, "Creating a Lively Academic Community," in Gamson et al., *Liberating Education*, 93–94.

33. A study on teachers who were effective in teaching adult students found that characteristically the teachers saw themselves—and presented themselves to the students—as learners rather than experts. They viewed and taught their subject matter as a resource for students' own lives rather than as an end in itself. See Carol Schneider, George O. Klemp, and Susan Kastendiek, *The Balancing Act: Competencies of Effective Teachers and Mentors in Degree Programs for Adults* (Chicago: University of Chicago Office of Continuing Studies, 1981).

34. "Educating Faculty for Teaching in an Interdisciplinary General Education Sequence" (forthcoming), 6–7; draft supplied by author.

35. Jerry Gaff, *New Life for the College Curriculum* (San Francisco: Jossey-Bass, 1991), 103.

36. The observations in this section were made during site visits (described in the Introduction) by the author and by Carol Schneider during the fall of 1991.

37. Presentation at AAC conference on "Reforming the Major," Philadelphia, 23 February 1992.

38. Presentation at Engaging Cultural Legacies symposium, "Designing Core Programs in the Humanities," Washington, D.C., 12 January 1992, and personal communication.

39. Butler, "Difficult Dialogue."

40. Mary H. Beaven and Gaston A. Mendoza, "The Influence of Black Authors on College Students in a Core Curriculum" (unpublished manuscript, Fairleigh Dickinson University, College of Business Administration, Teaneck Campus).

41. Presentation at Engaging Cultural Legacies symposium, "Designing Core Programs in the Humanities," Washington, D.C., 12 January 1992.

Selected Annotated Bibliography

Undergraduate curriculum

Association of American Colleges. *The Challenge of Connecting Learning.* Liberal Learning and the Arts and Sciences Major, Volume One. Washington: AAC, 1991.

> This report, the first in a three-volume series on the liberal arts major, was undertaken collaboratively with twelve national learned societies. It calls for each major course of study to be coherent; have a beginning, a structured middle, and a culminating experience at the end; and forge connections with general education, the interests of students, and societal issues.

_____. *Integrity in the College Curriculum: A Report to the Academic Community.* Washington: AAC, 1985.

> This report laments the supermarket approach found in undergraduate curricula, calls on "the faculty as a whole to accept responsibility for the curriculum as a whole," and recommends a minimum required curriculum for all students.

Boyer, Ernest L. *College: The Undergraduate Experience in America.* New York: Harper & Row, 1987.

> This book provides a comprehensive look at undergraduate education drawing on national surveys of students and faculty members. It contains useful analyses and suggestions concerning the curriculum, faculty, and students as well as whole institutions. Boyer argues that general education and the academic major should be mutually reinforcing.

Boyer, Ernest L., and Arthur Levine. *A Quest for Common Learning.* Washington: Carnegie Foundation for the Advancement of Teaching, 1981.

> This volume argues that general-education revivals occur during times of social fragmentation and that general education functions to restore social bonds. Boyer and Levine recommend a core curriculum stressing concerns common to all people. Topics for a common core include the use of symbols, membership in groups and institutions, activities of production and consumption, relationships with nature, sense of time, and beliefs and values.

Cheney, Lynne V. *50 Hours: A Core Curriculum for College Students*. Washington: National Endowment for the Humanities, 1990.

> This booklet argues that all students—whatever their academic major or intended career—should take fifty semester hours of work in general education. This work should be spread among several content and skill areas which Cheney discusses with some specificity and illustrates through NEH-funded projects.

Gaff, Jerry G. "Avoiding the Potholes: Strategies for Reforming General Education." *Educational Record* 60 (Fall 1980): 50–59.

> This paper is a primer for faculty and administrative leaders of a curriculum reform process. It stresses the importance of following an effective process, identifies forty-three procedures used by curriculum committees that lead to potholes, and discusses alternative strategies that may be more successful.

_____. *New Life for the College Curriculum: Assessing Achievements and Furthering Progress in the Reform of General Education*. San Francisco: Jossey-Bass, 1991.

> The first section discusses the need for curriculum reform and describes emerging curriculum trends. The second section contains the results of a survey analyzing the consequences of changes in general education reported by campus leaders. Gaff offers suggestions for making general education more central to academic life.

Task Group on General Education. *A New Vitality in General Education*. Washington: AAC, 1988.

> General education is defined as "the knowledge, skills, and attitudes that all of us use and live by during most of our lives—whether as parents, citizens, lovers, travelers, participants in the arts, leaders, volunteers, or good samaritans." This monograph provides many examples of curricular alternatives, approaches to teaching and learning, and administrative support necessary for effective general education.

Zemsky, Robert. *Structure and Coherence: Measuring the Undergraduate Curriculum*. Washington: AAC, 1989.

> After studying more than twenty-five thousand student transcripts, Zemsky concludes that "there is a notable absence of structure and coherence in college and university curricula." This monograph discusses breadth and depth in light of the results.

Core Curriculum Reform

Allardyce, Gilbert. "The Rise and Fall of the Western Civilization Course." *American Historical Review* 87 (June 1982): 695–725.

> This article chronicles the history of the Western Civilization course in five institutions—Harvard University, the University of Chicago, the University of Massachusetts–Amherst, Stanford University, and Columbia University, "where Western Civ was purportedly 'invented' in 1919"—represented at an American Historical Association annual meeting session in 1976, at which William McNeill called for a "rebuilding of freshmen history on the general education ideal." This account of political interests helps put today's discussions of "what every student should know" in context. See also Carolyn Lougee's "Comment" on pages 726–729, which speaks to the necessity of developing introductory courses that are interdisciplinary and inter-cultural, "reflecting a more humane set of power relationships, an updated nonassimilationist model of cultures."

Campbell, John, and Thomas Flynn. "Can Colleges Go Back to a Core Curriculum?" *Planning for Higher Education* 19 (Fall 1990): 9–16.

> Today's core curriculum must be rooted in each institution's own aca-demic focus, its special mission, and the kinds of students it enrolls. The authors describe the process of creating the sixty-one-hour core curriculum at Mount Saint Mary's College (Md.)—which includes a two-year integrated sequence in Western civilization and a require-ment in non-Western studies—and draw helpful lessons for those planning new core curricula.

Moseley, Merritt. "Educating Faculty for Teaching in an Interdisciplinary General Education Sequence." (forthcoming).

> This article highlights useful approaches to training faculty members to teach in general-education courses. The author draws on strategies that have worked in the University of North Carolina–Asheville's four-course, sixteen-hour, interdisciplinary core Humanities Program.

Schneider, Carol G. "Engaging Cultural Legacies: A Multidimensional Endeavor." *Liberal Education* 77 (May/June 1991): 2–7.

> This introduction to a special issue of AAC's journal on AAC's Cultural Legacies project describes three discernible trends in intel-lectual strategies to engage cultural multiplicity in core programs: dif-ference; exploring texts in context; and dialogue with contemporary culture. This issue also contains brief reports on the core programs at seventeen of the sixty-three institutions participating in the Cultural Legacies project.

Cultural Pluralism/Diversity

Adams, Maurianne, ed. *Diversity in the College Classroom*. New Directions for Teaching and Learning, no. 52. San Francisco: Jossey Bass, 1992.
> Essays and articles in this volume present concrete examples of how faculty members can revise courses in diverse curricula to include multicultural issues effectively.

Association of American Colleges and National Women's Studies Association. *Liberal Learning and the Women's Studies Major*. College Park, Md.: NWSA, 1991.
> This report describes the history of women's studies as an academic field: its dramatic growth, increasing influence, and tensions within the current structure of higher education. It discusses the intellectual goals of women's studies, the structure of the women's studies major, and student-centered pedagogies.

Butler, Johnnella E., and Walter, John C., eds. *Transforming the Curriculum: Ethnic Studies and Women's Studies*. Albany: State University of New York Press, 1991.
> This collection of essays presents the theoretical underpinnings, teaching approaches, and resources of ethnic studies and women's studies that can be brought to bear on curriculum transformation. It is useful for both curriculum planning and course revision.

"Diversity on Campus." *Change* 23 (September/October 1991); "The Curriculum and Multiculturalism." *Change* 24 (January/February 1992).
> These two special issues focus on multicultural education. Articles cover topics such as the media, the curriculum, ethnic and women's studies, faculty development, student life, campus ethos, and national trends in diversity requirements.

Greene, Madeleine F., ed. *Minorities on Campus: A Handbook for Enhancing Diversity*. Washington: American Council on Education, 1989.
> This handbook identifies important principles that institutions must adopt in order to address diversity successfully and profiles successful programs, strategies, and resources. Curriculum planners will be most interested in the chapter on teaching, learning, and the curriculum.

Hill, Patrick J. "Multi-Culturalism: The Crucial Philosophical and Organizational Issues." *Change* 23 (July/August 1991): 39–47.

> Both those who deem higher education culpable for marginalizing the diversity of human experience and those who worry about fragmentation and "particularism" in the curriculum are concerned with the comparative value of diverse visions and how we are to conceive their relationship. Hill examines four major frameworks that have been used in the West to comprehend or order diversity and their ramifications for current and possible approaches to multiculturalism in the curriculum.

Liberal Education

> The following issues of AAC's journal focus on themes that are particularly relevant to incorporating cultural legacies, multicultural curricula, and general education.

> "Re-Centering: Papers from the 1992 Annual Meeting" (March/April 1992).

> "The International Campus" (November/December 1991)

> "Progressing from Debate to Dialogue" (September/October 1991)

> "Engaging Cultural Legacies" (May/June 1991)

> "Discussing Diversity" (January/February 1991)

> "Intellectual Community" (November/December 1990)

> "Connected Learning: Selected Papers from the 1989 Annual Meeting" (November/December 1989)

> "Intercultural Education" (September/October 1987)

Minnich, Elizabeth K. *Transforming Knowledge*. Philadelphia: Temple University Press, 1990.

> In a close philosophical analysis—from a feminist perspective—of traditional knowledge bases and paradigms, Minnich finds several classes of epistemological error: faulty generalization, circular reasoning, mystified concepts, and partial knowledge. She concludes that "we need to explore a much richer range of materials, lives, voices, and achievements" in order to correct these errors in presumed knowledge.

Schmitz, Betty. *Integrating Women's Studies into the Curriculum: A Guide and Bibliography*. New York: Feminist Press, 1985.

> A study of successful curricular change strategies used by colleges and universities integrating scholarship on and by women into general-education courses. The bibliography, while dated, contains many books of model syllabi that are still available.

Pedagogy

Association of American Colleges and National Women's Studies Association. *The Courage to Question: Women's Studies and Student Learning*. Washington: AAC, 1992.

> This volume describes the results of a three-year study assessing learning in women's studies courses at seven colleges and universities. Organized as a series of case studies with data from campus-based assessment designs, the research yields new insights about classroom dynamics, skills development, multicultural learning, and collaborative pedagogies.

Border, Laura L. B., and Chism, Nancy V. N., eds. *Teaching for Diversity*. New Directions for Teaching and Learning, no. 49. San Francisco: Jossey-Bass, 1992.

> This collection of essays uses discussions of communication styles, classroom interaction patterns, faculty development programs, and administrative strategies to illustrate how to improve teaching and learning in multicultural classrooms.

Gabelnick, Faith, Jean MacGregor, Robin S. Matthews, and Barbara Leigh Smith. *Learning Communities: Creating Connections Among Students, Faculty, and Disciplines*. New Directions for Teaching and Learning, no. 41. San Francisco: Jossey-Bass, 1990.

> Learning is an individual but not solitary activity, the authors argue; at its best it occurs in a community of learners. The authors describe various forms of learning communities, the advantages for faculty members and students, strategies for developing them, and some of their consequences.

Smith, Barbara Leigh, and MacGregor, Jean. "What is Collaborative Learning?" In *Collaborative Learning: A Sourcebook for Higher Education*, edited by Anne Goodsell, et al. Syracuse, N.Y.: National Center on Postsecondary Teaching, Learning, and Assessment, 1992.

> A comprehensive overview of the characteristics, assumptions, goals, and approaches of collaborative learning by two well-known pioneers in the field. This booklet makes distinctions among terms often confused with one another (cooperative learning, learning communities, learner-centered instruction, group work, and so forth) and provides definitions. Descriptions of successful programs are included.

Weaver, Frederic S. *Liberal Education: Critical Essays on Professions, Pedagogy, and Structure*. New York: Teachers College Press, 1991.

> Critical inquiry in the liberal arts and sciences—not coverage of subject matter—is held to be the central element of undergraduate edu-

cation. Weaver explores the implications of this approach for teaching in a number of areas, including African American studies, teacher education, faculty development, academic advising, and writing about teaching.

Student Outcomes

Astin, Alexander W. *What Matters in College?: Four Critical Years Revisited.* San Francisco: Jossey-Bass, 1992.

In exploring the relations between outcomes in college and features of the educational environment, Astin concludes that peer involvement and student-teacher interaction are far more significant in shaping persistence and achievement than curricular structure or particular content. Based on this and earlier research, Astin strongly endorses collaborative and other forms of active student learning.

_____. "Involvement: The Cornerstone of Excellence." *Change* 17 (July/August 1985): 35–39.

Excellence often is defined in terms of resources (physical plant, library volumes, endowment) or reputation (faculty research, student test scores, graduates earning advanced degrees). Excellence in education, however, ought to mean developing the talent of students, indicated by the "value added" to the student by the college. Research shows that student involvement in the academic enterprise—in all of its forms—is the most powerful educational force.

Hutchings, Patricia, and Theodore Marchese. "Watching Assessment: Questions, Stories, Prospects." *Change* 22 (September/October 1990): 12–38.

"Assessment is best understood as *a set of questions*," largely about student learning. This article contains institutional vignettes, state trends, methods of assessment, anecdotes, war stories, cautionary tales, and speculations about prospects.

Pascarella, Ernest T., and Patrick T. Terenzini. *How College Affects Students.* San Francisco: Jossey-Bass, 1991.

A comprehensive synthesis of more than 2,600 studies of the effects of college on a variety of college outcomes, ranging from cognitive, moral, and attitudinal development through socioeconomic attainment and the quality of life. The authors report that "evidence unequivocally indicates that greater content learning and cognitive development occur in classrooms where students are engaged in and by the instructional…processes."